WE ARE THE DEAD

Ruined Country – Old Battlefield, Vimy, near La Folie Wood (1918)
Paul Nash (1889–1946)

We Are The Dead

Poems and Paintings from the Great War
1914–1918

SELECTED AND INTRODUCED BY DAVID ROBERTS

THE RED HORSE PRESS

Published by The Red Horse Press
www.redhorsepress.co.uk

Introduction © David Roberts 2012
First published 2012
ISBN 978 1 908916 19 8

Concept and design © Bookcraft Ltd 2012
www.bookcraft.co.uk

Project managed by John Button
Designed by Lucy Guenot
Editorial and rights management by Julie Laws

Set in Plantin

A CIP catalogue record for this book is available from the British Library.

5 4 3 2 1

Printed in Singapore by Imago

Contents

POEMS BY IRISH WRITERS

Poems by Australian writers

Poems by Canadian writers

POEMS BY FRENCH WRITERS

POEMS BY GERMAN WRITERS

INTRODUCTION

DAVID ROBERTS

In the opening years of the twentieth century the world was changing dramatically. Some poets felt that the archaic language and strict verse forms often associated with writing poetry were no longer adequate or appropriate in what was now being recognised as a 'modern' world. Some, such as Guillaume Apollinaire in France, were excited by what seemed to be a plethora of modern inventions, including the motor car, photography, cinema, mass circulation newspapers and the aeroplane. The world was new and good and exhilarating. Apollinaire decided that a complete revolution in the use of words was necessary.

In contrast, and at the same time, European powers were developing their arms industries and military power. Popular literature was full of war talk; as a reaction, at least in Germany, France and Britain, important pacifist movements were established.

In 1914 the Great War erupted, and across Europe patriotism and militarism were encouraged by politicians, priests and newspaper proprietors. A popular enthusiasm developed on all sides for war which, most people believed, would be short, glorious and victorious. Newspapers and magazines welcomed and published hundreds of poems that celebrated the military prowess of each country, and portrayed the war as a war of right against wrong and every soldier as a hero. Across France, Germany and Britain many thousands of poems of this type were written by hundreds of previously unknown writers. In Canada and Australia, also, large numbers of jingoistic pro-war poems were written. The vast majority of these poems had nothing to do with personal experience or insight, and little to do with reality. They were clichéd and bombastic. Their writers appear to have had no awareness of the carnage and suffering caused by modern warfare.

Some writers felt a deep and almost mystical, even religious, attraction to the idea of fighting and defending one's country. These included Rupert Brooke in Britain and, in France, Nicolas Beauduin and Jean-Pierre Calloc'h. In 1911 Brooke had been one of seventeen poets who called themselves Georgians who, to varying degrees, were trying to break away from the styles and confines of earlier poetry.

Alongside the new poets ardent for war were the establishment poets, who included, in Britain, Thomas Hardy, Robert Bridges and Rudyard Kipling, all of whom were enlisted in the secret war propaganda bureau run by Charles Masterman from an office in Buckingham Gate, London. The Canadian Charles G.D. Roberts who, early in the war, joined fellow countryman Max Aitken working on propaganda in London, wrote verse enthusing about the war. In Germany, Rainer Maria Rilke, as Germany's leading poet, did his best to write appropriate pro-war poetry. Whilst some of this poetry was written with conviction, even passion, some of the poetry produced by these writers may seem forced and hollow as we look back on it from the twenty-first century.

The responses of soldiers at the front, many of whom were facing or enduring industrialised warfare, was varied. The singing of cynical, ironic, anti-authoritarian and often crude songs was very popular. Many soldiers wrote poetry expressing a determination, whatever the cost, to see the war through to victory. Some celebrated war itself. Some wrote poems describing events or expressing a personal response to experiences. Amongst these were many who struggled to find words to express the enormity of the horror that they were enduring.

Wilfred Owen wrote that 'the true poet must be truthful'. It is the truthfulness to experience that distinguishes the best war poetry, together with a determination and talent to find the most powerful words to express experiences and responses – to tell the world the truth about what war was really like. These poets sought to be witnesses to the realities of war.

In Britain a small number of war poets, mainly soldiers who expressed their responses to frontline action, but also a few women writers who wrote about such things as civilian experiences of war and the trauma of losing loved ones, have become an important part of British culture. They are seen by many, for better or for worse, as the authentic voices, the true interpreters, of the Great War. They include Wilfred Owen, Siegfried Sassoon, Edward Thomas, Ivor Gurney, Isaac Rosenberg, Charles Sorley and Vera Brittain.

It might be imagined that war poets of the First World War in other countries would enjoy a similar status. However, in general non-British war poets are unknown in their own countries and, until now, have been almost completely unknown in Britain. The British view of the Great War has been seen almost entirely through the eyes of its native poets, with the result that the British appreciation of the Great War and its poetry has been one-sided and unduly narrow. This volume aims to widen understanding and appreciation of the war and its poetry by presenting a significant selection of poems by Irish, Australian, Canadian, French and German writers.

IRISH POETRY OF THE GREAT WAR

Those that I fight I do not hate,
Those that I guard I do not love;

W.B. Yeats, *An Irish Airman Foresees his Death*

In 1914 Ireland was part of Great Britain, but the Irish had more reason than most other nations fighting in the First World War to feel ambivalent about the role of their soldiers. During the First World War their main concerns were 'Why are we fighting?' and the 1916 rebellion against British rule.

Over the decades there had grown an increasingly strident movement within Ireland pressing for independence from Britain, and the question of independence was a burning issue. Within Ireland itself the Protestants wished to remain part of the British Empire. Feelings were running so high that both the Catholic south and the Protestant north, prior to the outbreak of war, had started to import weapons and ammunition from Germany in readiness to settle the dispute.

In the middle of the First World War, at Easter 1916, armed Irish Nationalists in the south seized the central post office and other key buildings in Dublin. After a week of fighting the rebels surrendered and over three thousand people were arrested, including sixteen of the leaders. Even though some of them had not been involved in the action, fifteen of them were executed by firing squad by the British.

In spite of anti-British feeling in Ireland, more than 210,000 Irishmen volunteered to serve in the British army and navy in the war. At least 49,400 of them were killed. The Irish regiments were renowned for their tenacity and bravery, and their sacrifice was great. When many of the Irish soldiers returned to their homes after the war they were regarded as traitors, and between 1919 and 1922 more than two hundred former soldiers were murdered.

Ironically, the Irish war poet who best captured the bitter sadness and mystery of the Irish men caught up in the First World War was the man who so famously condemned the whole idea of a poet writing war poetry, W.B. Yeats. He was greatly moved by the death of his friend, Robert Gregory, a pilot who was shot down and killed in Italy in a friendly-fire accident in January 1918. Yeats wrote four poems about this loss. *An Irish Airman Foresees his Death*, a poem of exceptional elegance, and *Reprisals* are included in this selection.

The War Artist (Self-Portrait) (1917)
William Orpen (1878–1931)

As an Irish patriot he felt duty bound to write about the Easter Uprising in *Easter 1916*, and it might be expected that his feelings on this topic would be clear. However, for personal reasons his feelings were mixed and muted. One might expect his regret and condemnation of the executions would be complete, but one of the men who was executed, Major John MacBride, he did not like. Furthermore, MacBride's wife was Maud Gonne, the woman Yeats so obsessively and for so long had wanted to marry. He proposed to her in the summer of 1916. It was his fifth and final rejection by her. Part of the strength of this poem is Yeats's honesty. He is not tempted to write a eulogy, painting flawed mortals with glowing praise. And, in the knowledge that England had promised some form of independence which he believed should be waited for, he disapproved of the rebellion. He mentions this, too, and quietly omits most of the names of those executed.

Initially Francis Ledwidge thought he would not fight in the war, but after much soul-searching he decided he would. 'I joined the British Army because she stood between Ireland and an enemy, and our civilisation and I would not have her say she defended us while we did nothing at home but pass resolutions.' In his poetry he celebrated his part in the war, and seemed to believe that he was fulfilling his Christian duty, fighting for liberty, justice, love and peace.

AUSTRALIAN POETRY OF THE GREAT WAR

In terms of geographical size Australia is the sixth largest country in the world, but at the start of the Great War, in terms of population – approximately five million people – it was one of the smallest. It was also a very new country. It gained independence in 1901 as a federation of formerly separate states, but only finally came together in 1911 when the Northern Territory and the Australian Capital Territory joined the federation. The war was, in essence, a European war, yet tens of thousands of ordinary citizens on the far side of the earth volunteered to come and fight, so risking their lives. There were almost 417,000 men and 2,000 women volunteers from Australia, with an eventual death toll of 61,519.

When Britain declared war against Germany on 4 August 1914 the declaration automatically included the commitment of Britain's colonies to the war. But other factors were major influences in the Australian enthusiasm for the war: most Australian citizens considered themselves part of Britain; many of them were new immigrants; and the parents or grandparents of many had come from Britain.

As the first Australian troops left for Britain early in November 1914, hostilities between Britain and Turkey (which sided with Germany) flared up. The Australians were diverted to Egypt to train, and defend the Suez Canal against the Turks. From here they departed for their attack on the Turkish mainland at Gallipoli on 25 April 1915. This was the start of a campaign that was to cost the Australians, New Zealanders (the ANZACS), and others, appalling suffering and loss in a campaign characterised by an unusual degree of military incompetence.

It was Australia's (and New Zealand's) baptism of fire as nations when courage, endurance and solidarity ('mateship' is the term used by Australians and New Zealanders) were tested to the limit. The date of that first attack is now Australia and New Zealand's 'ANZAC Day', a national holiday and a day of remembrance paralleled by 11 November, but it is also a day to celebrate national qualities of character and the day when Australia and New Zealand 'entered history'.

The departure of the troops from Gallipoli in December sealed an enduring sense of strength and tragedy. Gunner Frank Westbrook's poem, *Dawn before Anzac*, anticipates the first landing. Leon Gellert's poems, *Armageddon* and *The Last to Leave*, reflect on the battles and the evacuation.

From 1916 to 1918 the Australians played a very important role in France, both in making advances and suffering further huge losses. Australian troops also played a major role in the Allied capture of Palestine and the occupation of Syria and Lebanon.

The Australian poems in this volume convey the intense experience and spiritual impact of the participation of Australians in the Great War.

CANADIAN POETRY OF THE GREAT WAR

When Britain declared war against Germany, Canadian leaders were quick to give their wholehearted support. As in Australia, the recent immigrants from Britain and those descended from British immigrants were keen to lend their support for the war, but those of French origin were markedly more reluctant. Even so, within one month of the declaration of war over 32,000 volunteers had begun training. By the end of the war, Canada had sent to Europe 619,636 service personnel, including more than 3,000 nurses. Their courage, endurance and achievements are legendary. Over 67,000 Canadians were killed in the war.

As in other countries in the opening months of the war there was a profusion of expressions of patriotism, optimism and high moral calling for a battle of 'right against wrong', and with little sense of reality. Even the distinguished and prolific author Charles G.D. Roberts could seem seriously out of touch. He wrote of the Germans after the German seizure of the French town of Cambrai in August 1914, 'We scourged them with the scourge of swords', and much more in that vein.

Canadian poets 'at home' wrote of the innocent young recruits leaving for the front, of the heartbreak of farewells, of opposition to the war, of the impossibility of effectively commemorating the huge sacrifice young people had made.

The songs sung by Canadian soldiers were typically irreverent and self-deprecating soldiers' songs, but soldiers with poetic talent, such as Frederick George Scott and John McCrae, wrote with power about front-line experience.

John McCrae wrote his celebrated poem, *In Flanders Fields*, the day after he buried his friend Lieutenant Alexis Helmer. McCrae personally conducted the burial service, and in these circumstances it is not surprising that in the poem he should imagine the dead calling for the fight to continue. Today many people may think of this poem as an evocation of the poppy fields of Flanders, representing the blood of the dead rather than as a call to war.

Perhaps the most important of Canada's Great War poets is the best-selling author of popular verse, Robert Service, who worked as an ambulance driver in the front line in France. He saw the war at close quarters and his brother was killed there. Adopting the persona of 'a working man', Service, in his poem *The Stretcher Bearer*, expresses a revulsion at the nature of war, ending the poem with an appeal to Christ to bring it all to an end. *The Mourners* is a bleak poem which refers to 'the foul, corpse-cluttered plain' and imagines the sky filled with the faces of a million mourning women expressing 'fathomless despair'. In contrast, the poem *Pilgrims*, which is about

the bereaved visiting war graves, strikes a positive note. The dead have experienced 'a splendid release', and, ''twas joy in the dying. To know we were winning you Peace!.'

FRENCH POETRY OF THE GREAT WAR

When the long-running animosities among the European empires, propaganda, provocations, miscalculations and fears, whipped up by journalism and jingoism, finally culminated in war in the summer of 1914, France was prepared and had four million soldiers ready for action.

Pacifists and International Socialists were against war in principle, but when the French army was mobilised and the Germans marched through Belgium into northern France, virtually every French citizen united in a will to defeat the German invader. The Germans must never again enter Paris as they had in 1871. The seized provinces of Alsace and Lorraine, which had been under German rule since that time, must be returned.

Within the French parliament the pacifist-leaning socialists and all the other parties agreed to suspend their ideological differences to concentrate on national defence in an arrangement known as the Union Sacrée, or Sacred Union. This French government was formed during the early stages of the First World War to show national unity.

Many French saw themselves as exemplars of civilisation, defending it against barbarism. In the face of the massacres and the wanton destruction in Belgium they had a point, but as the German war poetry in this volume suggests the atrocities committed by the German army in Belgium were shocking even to many soldiers within its ranks.

As the years went by the death toll mounted and, for many, the deprivations increased. The stalemates, setbacks, and terrible losses endured in such campaigns as those of Gallipoli, the Somme, and Verdun challenged the confidence of leaders and ranks alike. Resolution faltered. Armies mutinied. The passion for war began to cool. By the end of the war France had lost one and a third million men.

In France at the outset of the Great War, as in Germany and Britain, hundreds of war poets wrote enthusiastic verse with endlessly repeated, impersonal and very similar messages of support for the war. However, a great many talented and impressive poets, mostly unknown in France today, responded to the war in deeply thoughtful and often complex ways.

Guillaume Apollinaire is the best-known and most remarkable of the French war poets. As a writer, even before the war, he was an iconoclast, an innovator, extremely varied in his interests, enthusiasms and modes of expression. As a poet he abandoned punctuation, and provided his readers with an exhilarating circus of images, ideas and events.

Born in Italy of Polish and Italian parents, he truly wanted to become French, and achieved French nationality after he volunteered to fight for the country he loved. He felt no animosity towards the Germans, and seems to have volunteered to fight out of a desire to be part of the excitement of war. He joined the artillery and loved the sight of flares and explosions. Later he transferred to the infantry, suffered in gas attacks and, when shrapnel pierced his skull in 1916, was put out of the war for good. He died of the Spanish 'flu in 1918.

His war poetry expresses his initial excitement when he volunteered to fight, followed by a growing disenchantment with war as the years went by. His poem *The Little Car* has a visionary quality, imagining a total change in human existence and a monstrous abuse of humanity and human talent, all seen as a spectacular show mounted by a prodigiously wealthy entrepreneur. This show might, nevertheless, lead to better human understanding. All these ideas boil up within Apollinaire's uninhibited imagination.

Whilst virtually all French poets regretted war, there were a number who protested strongly against it. These include Edmund Adam, Henriette Sauret and Marc de Larreguy de Civrieux, who volunteered to fight but then wrote some very hard-hitting anti-war verse. René Arcos, who fought in the war before being invalided out, also wrote powerful pacifist poetry.

GERMAN POETRY OF THE GREAT WAR

The Germans had a tradition of writing war poetry long before the First World War, being a nation for whom war was a major interest and concern, with a highly militarised society going back to before the days of Frederick the Great. They had achieved a massive build-up of armaments in the opening years of the twentieth century, and had developed a highly-trained army of four and a half million men.

The Kaiser had made plain his desire to expand the German Empire, and had started to make moves to increase Germany's influence beyond Europe.

The German press and popular literature were full of war talk. Issues of war and peace were a concern to thinking Germans and, perhaps as a reaction to the media coverage of war issues, a pacifist movement developed. One of the voices of this movement was *Die Aktion*, a weekly revolutionary magazine first published in 1911. This was vehemently anti-patriotic, and published anti-war poets including Alfred Lichtenstein, Wilhelm Klemm and Hugo Ball. The last of these had volunteered to fight but, declared unfit for military service, had visited Belgium at the start of the war to see for himself what was going on. He was deeply shocked by the abuse of a neutral country which Germany had pledged to defend, and began writing against the war. Like many, he remained a true patriot whilst at the same time vigorously opposing the slaughter. Because of censorship he published much of his writing from Switzerland.

At the start of the war there was a swaggering general belief in the military power of the country, and thousands of poems celebrated Germany's warrior prowess. The most accomplished of these poets was Rainer Maria Rilke, who wrote of the war with a strange detachment, celebrating 'the war God in his Crimson heaven'. In a second poem about the war he speaks of 'a new creation which he (the God of War) animates with death'.

Some of Germany's poets, even from the first months of the war, were sickened by the violence, a revulsion which began long before that trend developed among British writers. Even before the war started, Georg Trakl had been a poet obsessed with what he saw as the spiritual decline of a civilisation overwhelmed by materialism. The war therefore came to him as a terrible confirmation of the truth of his fears, and his war experience led him to suicide.

August Stramm, an officer noted for his leadership and decorated for his bravery, experienced war in all its intensity and was shocked to the core by it. He wrote in October 1914, 'Words fail me with horror … I have no faith … where are the words to express what we are going through?' Like Wilfred Owen, he seems to have felt himself spiritually destroyed by all the killing, yet, at the same time, compelled to continue fighting. His poems tend to be not 'emotions recollected in tranquillity', but experiences expressed with great intensity in the here and now with a sort of stammering incoherence and the use of neologisms not normally encountered in poetry. He died on 1 September 1915 leading his company in an assault across a canal.

Alfred Lichtenstein wrote in an entirely different manner. To him the whole idea of the war was preposterous. He could not take it seriously and so wrote in a tragic, flippant manner. In October 1913 he had begun his year's compulsory military service. His response to this, and to the war when it came, was that of a fool or court jester, the one who appears to be saying things for a laugh but is often speaking the truth that no one else dare speak. In one poem, *Leaving for the Front*, he joked that maybe in thirteen days he would be dead. In fact he lived for a further seven weeks. Involved in fierce fighting during the Battle of Saarburg he suddenly became deadly serious. *The Battle at Saarburg* was his last poem before his death on 25 September 1914 at the age of 25.

The small selection of poems in this volume will give the reader some idea of the intensity of feeling, the range of thought and the accomplishment of German poets of the Great War.

FIRST WORLD WAR ARTISTS

The innovative idea behind this anthology is, for the first time, to place side by side the creative insights of poets and war artists from some of the main belligerent nations of the First World War.

The poets, whether civilian or military personnel, were almost all writing from a personal motive to express and describe their experiences and feelings in response to the war. Only a small number were working as propagandists. The artists, on the other hand, were mainly officially appointed by governments or employed by journals. As a result, the feelings and personal opinions of the artists are often more subtly expressed. They may be inferred from the moods of the paintings and from the styles adopted by the artists – expressionists with their emotionally charged colours and brushstrokes; futurists with their stylised mechanisation of the human form. Often they were limited in their powers to interpret the war by the subject matter they were required to record.

In the vast body of paintings of the First World War, portraits of members of the higher ranks in the armies, scenes of damaged buildings, and distant views of battle landscapes are common. Scenes of destruction, the machinery of war, explosions, weary soldiers and sad people are plentiful, but many artists, especially when 'official artists', did little to convey the scale of the suffering and the vast number of people killed in this war.

An attempt has been made in this book to associate paintings with the subject matter of particular poems. To match poems with paintings in any precise way would be a difficult task. In trying to achieve some connection between paintings and poems we have sometimes used a painting by a national of one country alongside a poem by a national of another country. At times the link between painting and poem is either tenuous or even non-existent. What we *can* claim is that the paintings provide a fascinating, impressive, wide-ranging, powerful and enlightening insight into the First World War, especially when seen alongside the poetry of the war.

Whilst some of the paintings included in this volume will be familiar, such as John Singer Sargent's 'Gassed, 1919', many have been lost to public view, hidden away in the vaults of museums and other archives for the best part of a hundred years.

John McCrae coined the expression, 'We are the Dead', but many of the poets and artists represented in this anthology did not die in the war. Most suffered greatly, however, and many were profoundly affected by it. Some questioned how allegedly civilised countries could bring about the war's unprecedented death toll, and such material, financial and spiritual destruction. The aftermath of the war, and the tragically misconceived Treaty of Versailles, presented survivors with a world of bewildering challenges. The survivors were alive, but were not experiencing life as they knew it before the war. They were changed, and their world was changed.

Some of the war artists, like some of the poets, felt that they must be a witness to the horrors of modern warfare which they found unacceptable. Paul Nash wrote to his wife of what he saw, 'it is unspeakable, godless, hopeless. I am no longer an artist interested and curious, I am a messenger who will bring back word from the men who are fighting to those who want the war to go on forever. Feeble, inarticulate, will be my message, but it will have a bitter truth, and may it burn their lousy souls.'

WAKE UP, ENGLAND

Robert Bridges

Thou careless, awake!
Thou peace-maker, fight!
Stand, England, for honour,
And God guard the Right!

Thy mirth lay aside,
Thy cavil and play:
The foe is upon thee,
And grave is the day.

The monarch Ambition
Hath harnessed his slaves;
But the folk of the Ocean
Are free as the waves.

For Peace thou art armed
Thy Freedom to hold:
Thy Courage as iron,
Thy Good-faith as gold.

Through Fire, Air, and Water
Thy trial must be:
But they that love life best
Die gladly for thee.

The Love of their mothers
Is strong to command:
The fame of their fathers
Is might to their hand.

Much suffering shall cleanse thee:
But thou through the flood
Shalt win to Salvation,
To Beauty through blood.

Up, careless, awake!
Ye peacemakers, Fight!
ENGLAND STANDS FOR HONOUR.
GOD DEFEND THE RIGHT!

Moonrise over Mametz Wood
William Thurston Topham (1888–1966)

PEACE

Rupert Brooke

Now, God be thanked Who has matched us with His hour,
    And caught our youth, and wakened us from sleeping,
With hand made sure, clear eye, and sharpened power,
    To turn, as swimmers into cleanness leaping,
Glad from a world grown old and cold and weary,
    Leave the sick hearts that honour could not move,
And half-men, and their dirty songs and dreary,
    And all the little emptiness of love!

Oh! we, who have known shame, we have found release there,
    Where there's no ill, no grief, but sleep has mending,
    Naught broken save this body, lost but breath;
Nothing to shake the laughing heart's long peace there
    But only agony, and that has ending;
    And the worst friend and
        enemy is but Death.

Le Cimetière de Châlons-sur-Marne
(The Cemetery of Châlons-sur-Marne)
(1917)
Félix Vallotton (1865–1925)

THE DEAD

Rupert Brooke

Blow out, you bugles, over the rich Dead!
    There's none of these so lonely and poor of old,
    But, dying, has made us rarer gifts than gold.
These laid the world away; poured out the red
Sweet wine of youth; gave up the years to be
    Of work and joy, and that unhoped serene,
    That men call age; and those who
        would have been,
Their sons, they gave, their immortality.

Blow, bugles, blow! They brought us,
        or our dearth,
    Holiness, lacked so long, and Love, and Pain.
Honour has come back, as a king, to earth,
    And paid his subjects with a royal wage;
And Nobleness walks in our ways again;
    And we have come into our heritage.

Regimental Band (c.1918)
Darsie Japp (1883–1973)

THE SOLDIER

Rupert Brooke

If I should die, think only this of me:
   That there's some corner of a foreign field
That is forever England. There shall be
   In that rich earth a richer dust concealed;
A dust whom England bore, shaped, made aware,
   Gave, once, her flowers to love, her ways to roam,
A body of England's, breathing English air,
   Washed by the rivers, blest by suns of home.

And think, this heart, all evil shed away,
   A pulse in the eternal mind, no less
   Gives somewhere back the thoughts by England given;
Her sights and sounds; dreams happy as her day;
   And laughter, learnt of friends; and gentleness,
In hearts at peace, under an English heaven.

A Gunner (1919)
Colin Unwin Gill (1892–1940)

MEN WHO MARCH AWAY (SONG OF THE SOLDIERS)

Thomas Hardy

What of the faith and fire within us
   Men who march away
   Ere the barn-cocks say
   Night is growing grey,
To hazards whence no tears can win us;
What of the faith and fire within us
   Men who march away!

Is it a purblind prank, O think you,
   Friend with the musing eye
   Who watch us stepping by,
   With doubt and dolorous sigh?
Can much pondering so hoodwink you?
Is it a purblind prank, O think you,
   Friend with the musing eye?

Nay. We see well what we are doing,
   Though some may not see —
   Dalliers as they be —
   England's need are we;
Her distress would leave us rueing:
Nay. We well see what we are doing,
   Though some may not see!

In our heart of hearts believing
   Victory crowns the just,
   And that braggarts must
   Surely bite the dust,
Press we to the field ungrieving,
In our heart of hearts believing
   Victory crowns the just.

Hence the faith and fire within us
   Men who march away
   Ere the barn-cocks say
   Night is growing grey,
To hazards whence no tears can win us;
Hence the faith and fire within us
   Men who march away.

Returning to the Trenches (1914)
C.R.W. Nevinson (1889–1946)

FOR ALL WE HAVE AND ARE

Rudyard Kipling

For all we have and are,
For all our children's fate,
Stand up and take the war,
The Hun is at the gate!
Our world has passed away,
In wantonness o'erthrown.
There is nothing left today
But steel and fire and stone!
    Though all we knew depart,
    The old Commandments stand: —
    'In courage keep your heart,
    In strength lift up your hand.'

Once more we hear the word
That sickened earth of old: —
'No law except the Sword
Unsheathed and uncontrolled.'
Once more it knits mankind,
Once more the nations go
To meet and break and bind
A crazed and driven foe.

Comfort, content, delight,
The ages' slow-bought gain,
They shrivelled in a night.
Only ourselves remain
To face the naked days
In silent fortitude,
Through perils and dismays
Renewed and re-renewed.
    Though all we made depart,
    The old Commandments stand: —
    'In patience keep your heart,
    In strength lift up your hand.'

No easy hope or lies
Shall bring us to our goal,
But iron sacrifice
Of body, will, and soul.
There is but one task for all —
One life for each to give.
What stands if Freedom fall?
Who dies if England live?

AUGUST 1914

Isaac Rosenberg

What in our lives is burnt
In the fire of this?
The heart's dear granary?
The much we shall miss?

Three lives hath one life —
Iron, honey, gold.
The gold, the honey gone —
Left is the hard and cold.

Iron are our lives
Molten right through our youth.
A burnt space through ripe fields,
A fair mouth's broken tooth.

*Sunshine and Dust Near Neuville St. Vaast –
A Scene on the British Lines of Communication (1918)*
E. Handley-Read (1870–1935)

DEAD MAN'S DUMP

Isaac Rosenberg

The plunging limbers over the shattered track

Racketed with their rusty freight,

Stuck out like many crowns of thorns,

And the rusty stakes like sceptres old

To stay the flood of brutish men

Upon our brothers dear.

The wheels lurched over sprawled dead

But pained them not, though their bones crunched.

Their shut mouths made no moan.

They lie there huddled, friend and foeman,

Man born of man, and born of woman,

And shells go crying over them

From night till night and now.

Earth has waited for them

All the time of their growth

Fretting for their decay:

Now she has them at last!

In the strength of their strength

Suspended — stopped and held.

Finale (Dead Soldiers) (1918)
Albin Egger-Lienz (1868–1926)

What fierce imaginings their dark souls lit?
Earth! have they gone into you?
Somewhere they must have gone,
And flung on your hard back
Is their soul's sack,
Emptied of God-ancestralled essences.
Who hurled them out? Who hurled?

None saw their spirits' shadow shake the grass,
Or stood aside for the half used life to pass
Out of those doomed nostrils and the doomed mouth,
When the swift iron burning bee
Drained the wild honey of their youth.

What of us, who flung on the shrieking pyre,
Walk, our usual thoughts untouched,
Our lucky limbs as on ichor fed,
Immortal seeming ever?
Perhaps when the flames beat loud on us,
A fear may choke in our veins
And the startled blood may stop.

The air is loud with death;
The dark air spurts with fire;
The explosions ceaseless are.
Timelessly now, some minutes past,
Those dead strode time with vigorous life,
Till the shrapnel called 'An end!'
But not to all. In bleeding pangs
Some borne on stretchers dreamed of home,
Dear things, war-blotted from their hearts.

A man's brains splattered on
A stretcher-bearer's face;
His shook shoulders slipped their load,
But when they bent to look again
The drowning soul was sunk too deep
For human tenderness.

They left this dead with the older dead,
Stretched at the cross roads.
Burnt black by strange decay
Their sinister faces lie,
The lid over each eye,
The grass and coloured clay
More motion have than they,
Joined to the great sunk silences.

Here is one not long dead;
His dark hearing caught our far wheels,
And the choked soul stretched weak hands
To reach the living word, the far wheels said,
The blood-dazed intelligence beating for light,
Crying through the suspense of the far
  torturing wheels
Swift for the end to break,
Or the wheels to break,
Cried as the tide of the world broke over his sight.

Will they come? Will they ever come?
Even as the mixed hoofs of the mules,
The quivering-bellied mules,
And the rushing wheels all mixed
With his tortured upturned sight.
So we crashed round the bend,
We heard his weak scream,
We heard his very last sound,
And our wheels grazed his dead face.

Gassed and Wounded (1918)
Eric Henry Kennington (1888–1960)

RETURNING, WE HEAR THE LARKS

Isaac Rosenberg

Sombre the night is.
And though we have our lives, we know
What sinister threat lurks there.

Dragging these anguished limbs, we only know
This poison-blasted track opens on our camp —
On a little safe sleep.

But hark! joy — joy — strange joy.
Lo! heights of night ringing with unseen larks
Music showering on our upturned list'ning faces.

Death could drop from the dark
As easily as song —
But song only dropped,
Like a blind man's dreams on the sand
By dangerous tides,
Like a girl's dark hair for she dreams no ruin lies there,
Or her kisses where a serpent hides.

The Ypres Salient at Night
(1918)
Paul Nash (1889–1946)

ALL THE HILLS AND VALES ALONG

Charles Sorley

All the hills and vales along
Earth is bursting into song,
And the singers are the chaps
Who are going to die perhaps.
    O sing, marching men,
    Till the valleys ring again.
    Give your gladness to earth's keeping,
    So be glad, when you are sleeping.

Cast away regret and rue,
Think what you are marching to.
Little live, great pass.
Jesus Christ and Barabbas
Were found the same day.
This died, that went his way.
    So sing with joyful breath,
    For why, you are going to death.
    Teeming earth will surely store
    All the gladness that you pour.

Earth that never doubts nor fears,
Earth that knows of death, not tears,
Earth that bore with joyful ease
Hemlock for Socrates,

Earth that blossomed and was glad
'Neath the cross that Christ had,
Shall rejoice and blossom too
When the bullet reaches you.
    Wherefore, men marching
    On the road to death, sing!
    Pour your gladness on earth's head,
    So be merry, so be dead.

From the hills and valleys earth
Shouts back the sound of mirth,
Tramp of feet and lilt of song
Ringing all the road along.
All the music of their going,
Ringing swinging glad song-throwing,
Earth will echo still, when foot
Lies numb and voice mute.
    On, marching men, on
    To the gates of death with song.
    Sow your gladness for earth's reaping
    So you may be glad, though sleeping.
    Strew your gladness on earth's bed,
    So be merry, so be dead.

WHEN YOU SEE MILLIONS OF THE MOUTHLESS DEAD

Charles Sorley

When you see millions of the mouthless dead

Across your dreams in pale battalions go,

Say not soft things as other men have said,

That you'll remember. For you need not so.

Give them not praise. For, deaf, how should they know

It is not curses heaped on each gashed head?

Nor tears. Their blind eyes see not your tears flow.

Nor honour. It is easy to be dead.

Say only this, 'They are dead.' Then add thereto,

'Yet many a better one has died before.'

Then, scanning all the o'ercrowded mass, should you

Perceive one face that you loved heretofore,

It is a spook. None wears the face you knew.

Great death has made all his for evermore.

Dead Germans in a Trench (1918)
William Orpen (1878–1931)

FOR THE FALLEN

Laurence Binyon

With proud thanksgiving, a mother for her children,
England mourns for her dead across the sea.
Flesh of her flesh they were, spirit of her spirit,
Fallen in the cause of the free.

Solemn the drums thrill; Death august and royal
Sings sorrow up into immortal spheres,
There is music in the midst of desolation
And a glory that shines upon our tears.

They went with songs to the battle, they were young,
Straight of limb, true of eye, steady and aglow.
They were staunch to the end against odds uncounted;
They fell with their faces to the foe.

They shall grow not old, as we that are left grow old:
Age shall not weary them, nor the years condemn.
At the going down of the sun and in the morning
We will remember them.

They mingle not with their laughing comrades again;
They sit no more at familiar tables of home;
They have no lot in our labour of the day-time;
They sleep beyond England's foam.

But where our desires are and our hopes profound,

Felt as a well-spring that is hidden from sight,

To the innermost heart of their own land they are known

As the stars are known to the Night;

As the stars that shall be bright when we are dust,

Moving in marches upon the heavenly plain;

As the stars that are starry in the time of our darkness,

To the end, to the end they remain.

Over the Top (1918)
John Nash (1893–1977)

AS THE TEAM'S HEAD-BRASS

Edward Thomas

As the team's head-brass flashed out on the turn

The lovers disappeared into the wood.

I sat among the boughs of the fallen elm

That strewed the angle of the fallow, and

Watched the plough narrowing a yellow square

Of charlock. Every time the horses turned

Instead of treading me down, the ploughman leaned

Upon the handles to say or ask a word,

About the weather, next about the war.

Scraping the share he faced towards the wood,

And screwed along the furrow till the brass flashed

Once more.

              The blizzard felled the elm whose crest

I sat in, by a woodpecker's round hole.

The ploughman said, 'When will they take it away?'

'When the war's over.' So the talk began —

One minute and an interval of ten,

A minute more and the same interval.

'Have you been out?' 'No.' 'And don't want to, perhaps?'

'If I could only come back again, I should.

I could spare an arm. I shouldn't want to lose

A leg. If I should lose my head, why, so,

I should want nothing more … Have many gone

From here?' 'Yes.' 'Many lost?' 'Yes, a good few.

Only two teams work on the farm this year.
One of my mates is dead. The second day
In France they killed him. It was back in March,
The very night of the blizzard, too. Now if
He had stayed here we should have moved the tree.'
'And I should not have sat here. Everything
Would have been different. For it would have been
Another world.' 'Ay, and a better, though
If we could see all all might seem good.' Then
The lovers came out of the wood again:
The horses started and for the last time
I watched the clods crumble and topple over
After the ploughshare and the stumbling team.

A Land Girl Ploughing (c.1918)
Cecil Aldin (1870–1935)

OUT IN THE DARK

Edward Thomas

Out in the dark over the snow
The fallow fawns invisible go
With the fallow doe;
And the winds blow
Fast as the stars are slow.

Stealthily the dark haunts round
And, when the lamp goes, without sound
At a swifter bound
Than the swiftest hound,
Arrives, and all else is drowned;

And star and I and wind and deer,
Are in the dark together, — near,
Yet far, — and fear
Drums on my ear
In that sage company drear.

How weak and little is the light,
All the universe of sight,
Love and delight,
Before the might,
If you love it not, of night.

Canadians in the Snow (1918)
James Morrice (1865–1924)

NIGHT PATROL

Arthur Graeme West

'Over the top! The wire's thin here, unbarbed
Plain rusty coils, not staked, and low enough:
Full of old tins, though — When you're through, all three,
Aim quarter left for fifty yards or so,
Then straight for that new piece of German wire;
See if it's thick, and listen for a while
For sounds of working; don't run any risks;
About an hour; now, over!'
                              And we placed
Our hands on the topmost sand-bags, leapt, and stood
A second with curved backs, then crept to the wire,
Wormed ourselves tinkling through, glanced back,
   and dropped.
The sodden ground was splashed with shallow pools,
And tufts of crackling cornstalks, two years old,
No man had reaped, and patches of spring grass.
Half-seen, as rose and sank the flares, were strewn
With the wreck of our attack: the bandoliers,
Packs, rifles, bayonets, belts, and haversacks,
Shell fragments, and the huge whole forms of shells
Shot fruitlessly — and everywhere the dead.
Only the dead were always present — present
As a vile sickly smell of rottenness;

The rustling stubble and the early grass,
The slimy pools — the dead men stank
   through all,
Pungent and sharp; as bodies loomed before,
And as we passed, they stank; then dulled away
To that vague foetor, all encompassing,
Infecting earth and air. They lay, all clothed,
Each in some new and piteous attitude
That we well marked to guide us back; as he,
Outside our wire, that lay on his back
   and crossed
His legs Crusader-wise; I smiled at that,
And thought of Elia and his Temple Church.
From him, at quarter left, lay a small corpse,
Down in a hollow, huddled as in bed,
That one of us put his hand on unawares.
Next was a bunch of half a dozen men
All blown to bits, an archipelago
Of corrupt fragments, vexing to us three,
Who had no light to see by, save the flares.
On such a trail, so light, for ninety yards
We crawled on belly and elbows, till we saw,
Instead of lumpish dead before our eyes,
The stakes and crosslines of the German wire.

We lay in shelter of the last dead man,
Ourselves as dead, and heard their shovels ring
Turning the earth, their talk and cough at times.
A sentry fired and a machine-gun spat;
They shot a glare above us, when it fell
And spluttered out in the pools of No Man's Land,

We turned and crawled past the remembered dead;
Past him and him, and them and him, until,
For he lay some way apart, we caught the scent
Of the Crusader and slide past his legs,
And through the wire and home, and got our rum.

Over the Top, Neuville-Vitasse (1918)
Alfred Bastien (1873–1955)

THE TARGET

Ivor Gurney

I shot him, and it had to be
One of us! 'Twas him or me.
'Couldn't be helped,' and none can blame
Me, for you would do the same.

My mother, she can't sleep for fear
Of what might be a-happening here
To me. Perhaps it might be best
To die, and set her fears at rest.

For worst is worst, and worry's done.
Perhaps he was the only son …
Yet God keeps still, and does not say
A word of guidance any way.

Well, if they get me, first I'll find
That boy, and tell him all my mind,
And see who felt the bullet worst,
And ask his pardon, if I durst.

All's a tangle. Here's my job.
A man might rave, or shout, or sob;
And God He takes takes no sort of heed.
This is a bloody mess indeed.

5th Marines at Champagne (1918)
John W. Thomason, Jr (1893–1944)

DE PROFUNDIS

Ivor Gurney

If only this fear would leave me I could dream of Crickley Hill,
   And a hundred thousand thoughts of home might comfort my heart in sleep;
But here the peace is shattered all day by the devil's will,
   And the guns bark night long to spoil the velvet silence deep.

O who could think that once he drank in quiet inns and cool,
   And saw brown oxen trooping the dry sands to slake
Their thirst at the river flowing, or plunged in a river pool
   To shake the sleepy drowse off before well awake?

We are stale here, we are covered body and soul and mind
   With mire of the trenches, close-clinging and foul,
We have left our old inheritance, our paradise behind,
   And clarity is lost to us, and cleanness of soul.

O blow here, you dusk-airs and breaths of half-light,
   And comfort despairs of your darlings that long
Night and day far through for sound of your bells or a sight
   Of your tree-bordered lanes, land of blossom and song.

Autumn will be here soon, but the road of coloured leaves
   Is not for us the up and down highway where go
Earth's pilgrims to wonder where Malvern upheaves
   That blue-emerald splendour under great clouds of snow.

Some day we'll fill the trenches, level the land. and turn

    Once more joyful faces to the country where trees

Bear thickly for good drink, where strong sunsets burn

    Huge bonfires of glory — O God, send us peace!

Hard it is for men of fens or moors to endure

    Exile and hardship, or the Northland grey-drear;

But we of the rich plain of sweet air and pure —

    O Death would take so much from us, how should we not fear?

Poperinghe: Two Soldiers (1918)
John Singer Sargent (1856–1925)

LAST LEAVE

Eileen Newton

Let us forget tomorrow! For tonight
At least, with curtains drawn, and driftwood piled
On our own hearthstone, we may rest, and see
The firelight flickering on familiar walls.
(How the blue flames leap when an ember falls!)

Peace, and content, and soul-security —
These are within. Without, the waste is wild
With storm-clouds sweeping by in furious flight,
And ceaseless beating of autumnal rain
Upon our window pane.

The dusk grows deeper now, the flames are low:
We do not heed the shadows, you and I,
Nor fear the grey wings of encroaching gloom,
So softly they enfold us. One last gleam
Flashes and flits, elusive as a dream,

And then dies out upon the darkened room.
So, even so, our earthly fires must die;
Yet, in our hearts, love's flame shall leap and glow
When this dear night, with all it means to me,
Is but a memory!

YWCA Hut for the Queen Mary's Army Auxiliary Corps, Le Havre
Beatrice Lithiby (1889–1966)

DOES IT MATTER?

Siegfried Sassoon

Does it matter? — losing your legs? …
For people will always be kind,
And you need not show that you mind
When others come in after hunting
To gobble their muffins and eggs.

Does it matter? — losing your sight? …
There's such splendid work for the blind;
And people will always be kind,
As you sit on the terrace remembering
And turning your face to the light.

Do they matter? — those dreams from the pit? …
You can drink and forget and be glad,
And people won't say that you're mad;
For they'll know you've fought for your country
And no one will worry a bit.

Memory of the Somme,
1 July 1916 (1916)
H. Russell (active 1914–1918)

THE GENERAL

Siegfried Sassoon

'Good-morning; good-morning!' the General said

When we met him last week on our way to the line.

Now the soldiers he smiled at are most of 'em dead,

And we're cursing his staff for incompetent swine.

'He's a cheery old card,' grunted Harry to Jack

As they slogged up to Arras with rifle and pack.

But he did for them both by his plan of attack.

The Old German Front Line, Arras (1916)
Charles Sims (1873–1928)

GREAT MEN

Siegfried Sassoon

The great ones of the earth
Approve, with smiles and bland salutes, the rage
And monstrous tyranny they have brought to birth.
The great ones of the earth
Are much concerned about the wars they wage,
And quite aware of what those wars are worth.

You Marshals, gilt and red,
You Ministers and Princes, and Great Men,
Why can't you keep your mouthings for the dead?
Go round the simple cemeteries; and then
Talk of our noble sacrifice and losses
To the wooden crosses.

*Captain R.W. Maude and Colonel du Tyl
in their Cellar in Amiens (1918)*
William Orpen (1878–1931)

MEMORIAL TABLET

Siegfried Sassoon

Squire nagged and bullied till I went to fight,
(Under Lord Derby's scheme). I died in hell —
(They called it Passchendaele).
  My wound was slight,
And I was hobbling back; and then a shell
Burst slick upon the duck-boards: so I fell
Into the bottomless mud, and lost the light.

At sermon-time, while Squire is in his pew,
He gives my gilded name a thoughtful stare;
For, though low down upon the list, I'm there;
'In proud and glorious memory' … that's my due.
Two bleeding years I fought in France, for Squire:
I suffered anguish that he's never guessed.
I came home on leave: and then went west …
What greater glory could a man desire?

*Canadian Gunners
in the Mud,
Passchendaele
(1917)*
Alfred Bastien
(1873–1955)

EVERYONE SANG

Siegfried Sassoon

Everyone suddenly burst out singing;

And I was filled with such delight

As prisoned birds must find in freedom,

Winging wildly across the white

Orchards and dark-green fields; on — on — and out of sight.

Everyone's voice was suddenly lifted;

And beauty came like the setting sun:

My heart was shaken with tears; and horror

Drifted away … O, but Everyone

Was a bird; and the song was wordless; the singing will never be done.

Home for Christmas (1918)
Frank Schoonover (1877–1972)

1914

Wilfred Owen

War broke: and now the Winter of the world
With perishing great darkness closes in.
The foul tornado, centred at Berlin,
Is over all the width of Europe whirled,
Rending the sails of progress. Rent or furled
Are all Art's ensigns. Verse wails. Now begin
Famines of thought and feeling. Love's wine's thin.
The grain of human Autumn rots, down-hurled.

For after Spring had bloomed in early Greece,
And Summer blazed her glory out with Rome,
An Autumn softly fell, a harvest home,
A slow grand age, and rich with all increase.
But now, for us, wild Winter, and the need
Of sowings for new Spring, and blood for seed.

The Field at Passchendaele (1918)
Paul Nash (1889–1946)

ANTHEM FOR DOOMED YOUTH

Wilfred Owen

What passing-bells for these who die as cattle?
   Only the monstrous anger of the guns.
   Only the stuttering rifles' rapid rattle
Can patter out their hasty orisons.
No mockeries now for them; no prayers nor bells,
   Nor any voice of mourning save the choirs, —
The shrill, demented choirs of wailing shells;
   And bugles calling for them from sad shires.

What candles may be held to speed them all?
   Not in the hands of boys, but in their eyes
Shall shine the holy glimmers of good-byes.
   The pallor of girls' brows shall be their pall;
Their flowers the tenderness of patient minds,
   And each slow dusk a drawing-down of blinds.

l'Enfer (1917)
Georges Paul Leroux (1877–1957)

DULCE ET DECORUM EST

Wilfred Owen

Bent double, like old beggars under sacks,
Knock-kneed, coughing like hags, we cursed
   through sludge,
Till on the haunting flares we turned our backs
And towards our distant rest began to trudge.
Men marched asleep. Many had lost their boots
But limped on, blood-shod. All went lame; all blind;
Drunk with fatigue; deaf even to the hoots
Of tired, outstripped Five-Nines that
   dropped behind.

Gas! Gas! Quick, boys! — An ecstasy of fumbling,
Fitting the clumsy helmets just in time;
But someone still was yelling out and stumbling,
And flound'ring like a man in fire or lime …
Dim, through the misty panes and thick
   green light,
As under a green sea, I saw him drowning.

In all my dreams, before my helpless sight,
He plunges at me, guttering, choking, drowning.

Gassed:
'In Arduis Fidelis'
(c.1919)
Gilbert Rogers
(*c.*1885–1940)

If in some smothering dreams you too could pace
Behind the wagon that we flung him in,
And watch the white eyes writhing in his face,
His hanging face, like a devil's sick of sin;
If you could hear, at every jolt, the blood
Come gargling from the froth-corrupted lungs,

Obscene as cancer, bitter as the cud
Of vile, incurable sores on innocent tongues, —
My friend, you would not tell with such high zest
To children ardent for some desperate glory,
The old Lie; Dulce et Decorum est
Pro patria mori.

Gassed (1918)
John Singer Sargent (1856–1925)

FUTILITY

Wilfred Owen

Move him into the sun —
Gently its touch awoke him once,
At home, whispering of fields unsown.
Always it woke him, even in France,
Until this morning and this snow.
If anything might rouse him now
The kind old sun will know.

Think how it wakes the seeds, —
Woke, once, the clays of a cold star.
Are limbs, so dear-achieved, are sides,
Full-nerved — still warm — too hard to stir?
Was it for this the clay grew tall?
— O what made fatuous sunbeams toil
To break earth's sleep at all?

Zonnebeke (1918)
William Orpen (1878–1931)

INSENSIBILITY

Wilfred Owen

I

Happy are men who yet before they are killed

Can let their veins run cold.

Whom no compassion fleers

Or makes their feet

Sore on the alleys cobbled with their brothers.

The front line withers.

But they are troops who fade, not flowers,

For poets' tearful fooling:

Men, gaps for filling:

Losses, who might have fought

Longer; but no one bothers.

II

And some cease feeling

Even themselves or for themselves.

Dullness best solves

The tease and doubt of shelling,

And Chance's strange arithmetic

Comes simpler than the reckoning of their shilling.

They keep no check on armies' decimation.

III

Happy are these who lose imagination:

They have enough to carry with ammunition.

Their spirit drags no pack.

Their old wounds, save with cold, can not more ache.

Having seen all things red,

Their eyes are rid

Of the hurt of the colour of blood for ever.

And terror's first constriction over,

Their hearts remain small-drawn.

Their senses in some scorching cautery of battle

Now long since ironed,

Can laugh among the dying, unconcerned.

IV

Happy the soldier home, with not a notion

How somewhere, every dawn, some men attack,

And many sighs are drained.

Happy the lad whose mind was never trained:

His days are worth forgetting more than not.

He sings along the march

Which we march taciturn, because of dusk,

The long, forlorn, relentless trend

From larger day to huger night.

The Harvest of Battle (1919)
C.R.W. Nevinson (1889–1946)

V

We wise, who with a thought besmirch
Blood over all our soul,
How should we see our task
But through his blunt and lashless eyes?
Alive, he is not vital overmuch;
Dying, not mortal overmuch;
Nor sad, nor proud,
Nor curious at all.
He cannot tell
Old men's placidity from his.

VI

But cursed are dullards whom no cannon stuns,
That they should be as stones.
Wretched are they, and mean
With paucity that never was simplicity.
By choice they made themselves immune
To pity and whatever mourns in man
Before the last sea and the hapless stars;
Whatever mourns when many leave these shores:
Whatever shares
The eternal reciprocity of tears.

STRANGE MEETING

Wilfred Owen

It seemed that out of battle I escaped
Down some profound dull tunnel, long since scooped
Through granites which titanic wars had groined.

Yet also there encumbered sleepers groaned,
Too fast in thought or death to be bestirred.
Then, as I probed them, one sprang up, and stared
With piteous recognition in fixed eyes,
Lifting distressful hands as if to bless.
And by his smile, I knew that sullen hall,
By his dead smile I knew we stood in Hell.

With a thousand pains that vision's face was grained;
Yet no blood reached there from the upper ground,
And no guns thumped, or down the flues
    made moan.
'Strange friend,' I said, 'here is no cause to mourn.'
'None,' said that other, 'save the undone years,
The hopelessness. Whatever hope is yours,
Was my life also; I went hunting wild
After the wildest beauty in the world,
Which lies not calm in eyes, or braided hair,
But mocks the steady running of the hour,
And if it grieves, grieves richlier than here.
For of my glee might many men have laughed,
And of my weeping something had been left,

Which must die now. I mean the truth untold,
The pity of war, the pity war distilled.
Now men will go content with what we spoiled,
Or, discontent, boil bloody, and be spilled.
They will be swift with swiftness of the tigress.
None will break ranks, though nations
    trek from progress.
Courage was mine, and I had mystery,
Wisdom was mine, and I had mastery:
To miss the march of this retreating world
Into vain citadels that are not walled.
Then, when much blood had clogged their
    chariot-wheels,
I would go up and wash them from sweet wells,
Even with truths that lie too deep for taint.
I would have poured my spirit without stint
But not through wounds; not on the cess of war.
Foreheads of men have bled where
    no wounds were.

I am the enemy you killed, my friend.
I knew you in this dark: for so you frowned
Yesterday through me as you jabbed and killed.
I parried; but my hands were loath and cold.
Let us sleep now … '

Paths of Glory (1917)
C.R.W. Nevinson (1889–1946)

REPORT ON EXPERIENCE
Edmund Blunden

I have been young, and now am not too old;
And I have seen the righteous forsaken,
His health, his honour and his quality taken.
　This is not what we were formerly told.

I have seen a green country, useful to the race,
Knocked silly with guns and mines, its villages vanished,
Even the last rat and the last kestrel banished —
　God bless us all, this was peculiar grace.

I knew Seraphina; Nature gave her hue,
Glance, sympathy, note, like one from Eden.
I saw her smile warp, heard her lyric deaden;
　She turned to harlotry; — this I took to be new.

Say what you will, our God sees how they run.
These disillusions are His curious proving
That He loves humanity and will go on loving;
　Over there are faith, life, virtue in the sun.

Blasted Trees
William Rothenstein (1872–1945)

INVALIDED

Edward Shilito

He limps along the city street,
Men pass him with a pitying glance;
He is not there, but on the sweet
And troubled plains of France.

Once more he marches with the guns,
Reading the way by merry signs,
His Regent Street through trenches runs,
His Strand among the pines.

For there his comrades jest and fight,
And others sleep in that fair land;
They call him back in dreams of night
To join their dwindling band.

He may not go; on him must lie
The doom, through peaceful years to live,
To have a sword he cannot ply,
A life he cannot give.

*Loading Wounded
at Boulogne (1919)*
John Hodgson Lobley
(1878–1954)

GERMAN PRISONERS

Joseph Lee

When first I saw you in the curious street,
Like some platoon of soldier-ghosts in grey,
My mad impulse was all to smite and slay,
To spit upon you — tread you 'neath my feet.
But when I saw how each sad soul did greet
My gaze with no sign of defiant frown,
How from tired eyes looked broken spirits down,
How each face showed the pale flag of defeat,

And doubt, despair and disillusionment,
And how were grievous wounds of many a head,
And on your garb red-faced was other red;
And how you stooped as men whose strength was spent,
I knew that we had suffered each as other,
And could have grasped your hand and cried,
   'My brother!'

German Prisoners (c.*1919*)
Frederick H. Varley (1881–1969)

WHEN I COME HOME

Lesley Coulson

When I come home, dear folk o' mine,
We'll drink a cup of olden wine;
And yet, however rich it be,
No wine will taste so good to me
As English air. How I shall thrill
To drink it in on Hampstead Hill
    When I come home!

When I come home, and leave behind
Dark things I would not call to mind,
I'll taste good ale and home-made bread,
And see white sheets and pillows spread.
And there is one who'll softly creep
To kiss me, ere I fall asleep,
And tuck me 'neath the counterpane,
And I shall be a boy again,
    When I come home!

When I come home from dark to light,
And tread the roadways long and white,
And tramp the lanes I tramped of yore,
And see the village greens once more,
The tranquil farms, the meadows free,
The friendly trees that nod to me,
And hear the lark beneath the sun,
'Twill be good pay for what I've done,
    When I come home!

Infantryman
H.E. Townsend (1879–1941)

THE RAINBOW

Lesley Coulson

I watch the white dawn gleam,
    To the thunder of hidden guns.
I hear the hot shells scream
Through skies as sweet as a dream
    Where the silver dawnbreak runs.
And stabbing of light
Scorches the virginal white.
But I feel in my being the old, high, sanctified thrill,
And I thank the gods that the dawn is beautiful still.

From death that hurtles by
    I crouch in the trench day-long,
But up to a cloudless sky
From the ground where our dead men lie
    A brown lark soars in song.
Through the tortured air,
Rent by the shrapnel's flare,
Over the troubleless dead he carols his fill,
And I thank the gods that the birds are beautiful still.

Where the parapet is low
    And level with the eye
Poppies and cornflowers glow
And the corn sways to and fro
    In a pattern against the sky.
The gold stalks hide
Bodies of men who died
Charging at dawn through the dew to be killed or to kill.
I thank the gods that the flowers are beautiful still.

When night falls dark we creep
    In silence to our dead.
We dig a few feet deep
And leave them there to sleep —
    But blood at night is red,
Yea, even at night,
And a dead man's face is white.
And I dry my hands, that are also trained to kill,
And I look at the stars — for the stars are beautiful still.

The Mule Track (1918)
Paul Nash (1889–1946)

But a Short Time to Live

Lesley Coulson

Our little hour — how swift it flies
When poppies flare and lilies smile;
How soon the fleeting minute dies,
Leaving us but a little while
To dream our dream, to sing our song,
To pick the fruit, to pluck the flower,
The Gods — they do not give us long —
One little hour.

Our little hour — how short it is
When Love with dew-eyed loveliness
Raises her lips for ours to kiss
And dies within our first caress.
Youth flickers out like wind-blown flame,
Sweets of today tomorrow sour,
For Time and Death, relentless, claim
Our little hour.

Our little hour — how short a time
To wage our wars, to fan our hates,
To take our fill of armoured crime,
To troop our banners, storm the gates.
Blood on the sword, our eyes blood-red,
Blind in our puny reign of power,
Do we forget how soon is sped
Our little hour?

Our little hour — how soon it dies:
How short a time to tell our beads,
To chant our feeble litanies,
To think sweet thoughts, to do good deeds.
The altar lights grow pale and dim,
The bells hang silent in the tower —
So passes with the dying hymn
Our little hour.

Somme Trench Poppies
Mary Riter Hamilton (1873–1954)

FROM THE SOMME

Lesley Coulson

In other days I sang of simple things,
  Of summer dawn, and summer noon and night,
The dewy grass, the dew-wet fairy rings,
  The lark's long golden flight.

Deep in the forest I made melody
  While squirrels cracked their hazel nuts on high,
Or I would cross the wet sand to the sea
  And sing to sea and sky.

When came the silvered silence of the night
  I stole to casements over scented lawns,
And softly sang of love and love's delight
  To mute white marble fauns.

Oft in the tavern parlour I would sing
  Of morning sun upon the mountain vine,
And, calling for a chorus, sweep the string
  In praise of good red wine.

I played with all the toys the gods provide,
  I sang my songs and made glad holiday.
Now I have cast my broken toys aside
  And flung my lute away.

A singer once, I now am fain to weep.
  Within my soul I feel strange music swell,
Vast chants of tragedy too deep — too deep
  For my poor lips to tell.

The Thinker on the Butte de Warlencourt (1918)
William Orpen (1878–1931)

NOON

Robert Nichols

It is midday: the deep trench glares …
A buzz and blaze of flies …
The hot wind puffs the giddy airs …
The great sun rakes the skies.

No sound in all the stagnant trench
Where forty standing men
Endure the sweat and grit and stench,
Like cattle in a pen.

Sometimes a sniper's bullet whirs
Or twangs the whining wire,
Sometimes a soldier sighs and stirs
As in hell's frying fire.

From out a high cool cloud descends
An aeroplane's far moan …
The sun strikes down, the thin cloud rends …
The black speck travels on.

And sweating, dizzied, isolate
In the hot trench beneath,
We bide the next shrewd move of fate
Be it of life or death.

Trônes Wood (1916)
Stanley Llewelyn Wood (1867–1928)

EVE OF ASSAULT
INFANTRY GOING DOWN TO TRENCHES

Robert Nichols

Downwards slopes the wild red sun.
We lie around a waiting gun;
Soon we shall load and fire and load.
But, hark! a sound beats down the road.

''Ello! wot's up?' 'Let's 'ave a look!'
'Come on, Ginger, drop that book!'
'Wot an 'ell of bloody noise!'
'It's the Yorks and Lancs, meboys!'

So we crowd: hear, watch them come —
One man drubbing on a drum,
A crazy, high mouth-organ blowing,
Tin cans rattling, cat-calls, crowing …

And above their rhythmic feet
A whirl of shrilling loud and sweet,
Round mouths whistling in unison;
Shouts: ''O's goin' to out the 'Un?'

'Back us up, mates!' 'Gawd, we will!'
''Eave them shells at Kaiser Bill!'
'Art from Lancashire, melad?'
'Gi' 'en a cheer, boys; make 'en glad.'
''Ip 'urrah!' 'Give Fritz the chuck.'
'Good ol' bloody Yorks!' 'Good-luck!'
'Cheer!'

      I cannot cheer or speak
Lest my voice, my heart must break.

Machine-gun (1915)
C.R.W. Nevinson (1889–1946)

THE DAY'S MARCH

Robert Nichols

The battery grides and jingles,
Mile succeeds to mile;
Shaking the noonday sunshine
The guns lunge out awhile,
And then are still awhile.

We amble along the highway;
The reeking, powdery dust
Ascends and cakes our faces
With a striped, sweaty crust.

Under the still sky's violet
The heat throbs on the air …
The white road's dusty radiance
Assumes a dark glare.

With a head hot and heavy,
And eyes that cannot rest,
And a black heart burning
In a stifled breast,

I sit in the saddle,
I feel the road unroll,
And keep my senses straightened
Toward tomorrow's goal.

There, over unknown meadows
Which we must reach at last,
Day and night thunders
A black and chilly blast.

Heads forget heaviness,
Hearts forget spleen,
For by that mighty winnowing
Being is blown clean.

Light in the eyes again,
Strength in the hand,
A spirit dares, dies, forgives,
And can understand!

And, best! Love comes back again
After grief and shame,
And along the wind of death
Throws a clean flame.

★ ★ ★

The battery grides and jingles,
Mile succeeds to mile;
Suddenly battering the silence
The guns burst out awhile …

★ ★ ★

I lift my head and smile.

Horse-drawn Transports
Passing the Cloth Hall, Ypres
(1917)
Gilbert Holiday (1879–1937)

DAWN ON THE SOMME

Robert Nichols

Last night rain fell over the scarred plateau,
And now from the dark horizon, dazzling, flies
Arrow on fire-plumed arrow to the skies,
Shot from the bright arc of Apollo's bow;
And from the wild and writhen waste below,
From flashing pools and mounds lit one by one,

Oh, is it mist, or are these companies
Of morning heroes who arise, arise
With thrusting arms, with limbs and hair aglow,
Toward the risen god, upon whose brow
Burns the gold laurel of all victories,
Hero and heroes' god, th' invincible Sun?

The Battle of Courcelette (1918)
Louis Weirter (1873–1932)

THE VICTORY BALL

Alfred Noyes

The cymbals crash,
    And the dancers walk,
With long silk stockings
    And arms of chalk,
Butterfly skirts,
    And white breasts bare,
And shadows of dead men
    Watching 'em there.

Shadows of dead men
    Stand by the wall,
Watching the fun
    Of the Victory Ball.
They do not reproach,
    Because they know,
If they're forgotten,
    It's better so.

Under the dancing
    Feet are the graves.
Dazzle and motley,
    In long bright waves,
Brushed by the palm-fronds
    Grapple and whirl
Ox-eyed matron,
    And slim white girl.

Fat wet bodies
    Go waddling by,
Girdled with satin,
    Though God knows why;
Gripped by satyrs
    In white and black,
With a fat wet hand
    On the fat wet back.

See, there is one child
    Fresh from school,
Learning the ropes
    As the old hands rule.
God, how the dead men
    Chuckle again,
As she begs for a dose
    Of the best cocaine.

'What did you think
    We should find,' said a shade,
'When the last shot echoed
    And peace was made?'
'Christ,' laughed the fleshless
    Jaws of his friend,
'I thought they'd be praying
    For worlds to mend,

'Making earth better,
    Or something silly,
Like whitewashing hell
    Or Piccadilly.
They've a sense of humour,
    These women of ours,
These exquisite lilies,
    These fresh young flowers!'

'Pish,' said a statesman
    Standing near,
'I'm glad they can busy
    Their thoughts elsewhere!
We mustn't reproach 'em.
    They're young, you see.'
'Ah,' said the dead men,
    'So were we!'

Victory! Victory!
    On with the dance!
Back to the jungle
    The new beasts prance!
God, how the dead men
    Grin by the wall,
Watching the fun
    Of the Victory Ball.

Anna Pavlova as a Bacchante (1911)
John Lavery (1856–1941)

ARMISTICE DAY, 1918

Robert Graves

What's all this hubbub and yelling,
  Commotion and scamper of feet,
With ear-splitting clatter of kettles and cans,
  Wild laughter down Mafeking Street?

O, those are the kids whom we fought for
  (You might think they'd been scoffing our rum)
With flags that they waved when we marched off to war
  In the rapture of bugle and drum.

Now they'll hang Kaiser Bill from a lamp-post,
  Von Tirpitz they'll hang from a tree …
We've been promised a 'Land Fit for Heroes' —
  What heroes we heroes must be!

And the guns that we took from the Fritzes,
  That we paid for with rivers of blood,
Look, they're hauling them down to Old Battersea Bridge
  Where they'll topple them, souse, in the mud!

But there's old men and women in corners
  With tears falling fast on their cheeks,
There's the armless and legless and sightless —
  It's seldom that one of them speaks.

And there's flappers gone drunk and indecent
  Their skirts kilted up to the thigh,
The constables lifting no hand in reproof
  And the chaplain averting his eye …

When the days of rejoicing are over,
  When the flags are stowed safely away,
They will dream of another wild 'War to End Wars'
  And another wild Armistice day.

But the boys who were killed in the trenches,
  Who fought with no rage and no rant,
We left them stretched out on their pallets of mud
  Low down with the worm and the ant.

The Fore-Cabin of HMS Queen Elizabeth *with
Admiral Beatty Reading the Terms of the Surrender of
the German Navy, Rosyth, November 16th, 1918.*
John Lavery (1856–1941)

PERHAPS

Vera Brittain

To R.A.L., who died of wounds in France, December 23rd, 1915

Perhaps some day the sun will shine again,
  And I shall see that still the skies are blue,
And feel once more I do not live in vain,
  Although bereft of You.

Perhaps the golden meadows at my feet
  Will make the sunny hours of spring seem gay,
And I shall find the white May-blossoms sweet,
  Though You have passed away.

Perhaps the summer woods will shimmer bright,
  And crimson roses once again be fair,
And autumn harvest fields a rich delight,
  Although You are not there.

Perhaps some day I shall not shrink in pain
  To see the passing of the dying year,
And listen to the Christmas songs again,
  Although You cannot hear.

But though kind Time may many joys renew,
  There is one greatest joy I shall not know
Again, because my heart for loss of You
  Was broken, long ago.

Youth Mourning (1916)
George Clausen (1852–1944)

FALLEN SUBALTERN

Herbert Asquith

The starshells float above, the bayonets glisten;
　We bear our fallen friend without a sound;
Below the waiting legions lie and listen
　To us, who march upon their burial-ground.

Wound in the flag of England, here we lay him;
　The guns will flash and thunder o'er the grave;
What other winding sheet should now array him,
　What other music should salute the brave?

As goes the Sun-god in his chariot glorious,
　When all his golden banners are unfurled,
So goes the soldier, fallen but victorious,
　And leaves behind a twilight in the world.

And those who come this way, in days hereafter,
　Will know that here a boy for England fell,
Who looked at danger with the eyes of laughter,
　And on the charge his days were ended well.

One last salute; the bayonets clash and glisten;
　With arms reversed we go without a sound:
One more has joined the men who lie and listen
　To us, who march upon their burial-ground.

The Second Battle of Ypres, April 22nd–May 25th, 1915 (1917)
Richard Jack (1866–1952)

NIGHTFALL

Herbert Asquith

Hooded in angry mist, the sun goes down:

Steel-grey the clouds roll out across the sea:

Is this a Kingdom? Then give Death the crown,

For here no emperor hath won, save He.

Void, 1918
Paul Nash (1889–1946)

FLOWER OF YOUTH

Katherine Tynan

Lest Heaven be thronged with grey-beards hoary,
  God, who made boys for His delight,
Stoops in a day of grief and glory
  And calls them in, in from the night.
When they come trooping from the war
Our skies have many a new gold star.

Heaven's thronged with gay and careless faces,
  New-waked from dreams of dreadful things,
They walk in green and pleasant places
  And by the crystal water-springs
Who dreamt of dying and the slain,
And the fierce thirst and the strong pain.

Dear boys! They shall be young for ever.
  The Son of God was once a boy.
They run and leap by a clear river
  And of their youth they have great joy.
God, who made boys so clean and good
Smiles with the eyes of fatherhood.

Now Heaven is by the young invaded;
  Their laughter's in the House of God.
Stainless and simple as He made it
  God keeps the heart o' the boy unflawed.
The old wise Saints look on and smile,
They are so young and without guile.

Oh! if the sonless mothers weeping,
  And widowed girls could look inside
The glory that hath them in keeping
  Who went to the Great War and died,
They would rise and put their mourning off,
And say: 'Thank God, he has enough!'

One of the Nelsons (1918)
Ambrose McEvoy (1878–1927)

THE MOTHER

Padraic Pearse

I do not grudge them: Lord, I do not grudge
My two strong sons that I have seen go out
To break their strength and die, they and a few,
In bloody protest for a glorious thing.
They shall be spoken of among their people,
The generations shall remember them,
And call them blessed;

But I will speak their names to my own heart
In the long nights;
The little names that were familiar once
Round my dead hearth.
Lord, thou art hard on mothers:
We suffer in their coming and their going;
And tho' I grudge them not, I weary, weary
Of the long sorrow — And yet I have my joy:
My sons were faithful, and they fought.

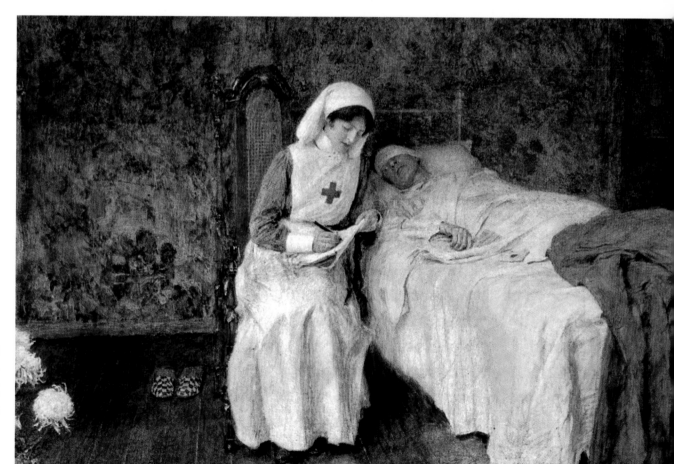

*The Last Message
(1918)*
William Hatherell
(1855–1928)

CONTINUITY

George 'AE' Russell

No sign is made while empires pass,
The flowers and stars are still His care,
The constellations hid in grass,
The golden miracles in air.

Life in an instant will be rent
Where death is glittering blind and wild —
The Heavenly Brooding is intent
To that last instant on Its child.

It breathes the glow in brain and heart,
Life is made magical. Until
Body and spirit are apart
The Everlasting works Its will.

In that wild orchid that your feet
In their next falling shall destroy,
Minute and passionate and sweet
The Mighty Master holds His joy.

Though the crushed jewels droop and fade
The Artist's labours will not cease,
And of the ruins shall be made
Some yet more lovely masterpiece.

Bourlon Wood, Somme (1918)
Ambrose McEvoy (1878–1927)

WASTE

George 'AE' Russell

All that heroic mood,
The will to suffer pain,
Were it on beauty spent,
An intellectual gain.

Had a fierce pity breathed
O'er wronged or fallen life,
Though strife had been unwise
We were not shamed by strife.

Had they but died for some
High image in the mind,
Not spilt the sacrifice
For words hollow as wind!

Darkened the precious fire,
The will we honour most
Spent in the waste! What sin
Against the Holy Ghost!

Portrait of a Youth
William Orpen (1878–1931)

STATESMEN

George 'AE' Russell

They tell us that they war on war. Why do they treat our wit with scorn?

The dragon from the dragon seed, the breed was true since life was born.

When has the lioness conceived the lamb beneath her tawny side?

When has the timid dove been born the offspring of the eagle's pride?

When Cherubim smite at their Light, oh! yes, we may believe this thing.

When Eblis risen in revolt casts from its shades their awful king.

We know how from the deeds men do a sudden blackness blinds the soul,

How kindled by their sacrifice lights up the instant aureole.

The thought, the deed, breed always true. Shall nations not the law obey?

Has not the Mighty Father store within His Treasure House to pay?

The noble and the base beget their kin, and empires
    ere they pass

See their own mirrored majesty arise within
    Time's looking-glass.

The pride that builded Babylon of Egypt was
    the mighty child:

The beauty of the Attic soul in many a lovely city smiled.

The empire that is built in pride shall call imperial pride
        to birth,

And with that shadow of itself must fight for empire
        of the earth.

Fight where ye will on earth or sea, beneath the wave,
        above the hills,

The foe ye meet is still yourselves, the blade ye forged
        the sword that kills.

*The Peace Conference at the
Quai d'Orsay (1919)*
William Orpen (1878–1931)

AFTER COURT MARTIAL

Francis Ledwidge

My mind is not my mind, therefore
I take no heed of what men say,
I lived ten thousand years before
God cursed the town of Nineveh.

The Present is a dream I see
Of horror and loud sufferings,
At dawn a bird will waken me
Unto my place among the kings.

And though men called me a vile name,
And all my dream companions gone,
'Tis I the soldier bears the shame,
Not I the king of Babylon.

The Vision of St George over the Battlefield (1915)
John Hassall (1868–1948)

LAMENT FOR THOMAS MCDONAGH

Francis Ledwidge

He shall not hear the bittern cry
In the wild sky, where he is lain,
Nor voices of the sweeter birds,
Above the wailing of the rain.

Nor shall he know when loud March blows
Thro' slanting snows her fanfare shrill,
Blowing to flame the golden cup
Of many an upset daffodil.

But when the Dark Cow leaves the moor,
And pastures poor with greedy weeds,
Perhaps he'll hear her low at morn
Lifting her horn in pleasant meads.

After an Attack
Austin Osman Spare (1886–1956)

SOLILOQUY

Francis Ledwidge

When I was young I had a care
Lest I should cheat me of my share
Of that which makes it sweet to strive
For life, and dying still survive,
A name in sunshine written higher
Than lark or poet dare aspire.

But I grew weary doing well.
Besides, 'twas sweeter in that hell,
Down with the loud banditti people
Who robbed the orchards, climbed the steeple
For jackdaws' eggs and made the cock
Crow ere 'twas daylight on the clock.
I was so very bad the neighbours
Spoke of me at their daily labours.

And now I'm drinking wine in France,
The helpless child of circumstance.
Tomorrow will be loud with war,
How will I be accounted for?

It is too late now to retrieve
A fallen dream, too late to grieve
A name unmade, but not too late
To thank the gods for what is great;
A keen-edged sword, a soldier's heart,
Is greater than a poet's art.
And greater than a poet's fame
A little grave that has no name.

The Cambrai Road (1918)
Maurice Cullen (1866–1934)

O'Connell Street

Francis Ledwidge

A noble failure is not vain
But hath a victory of its own.
A bright delectance from the slain
Is down the generations thrown.

And, more than Beauty understands,
Has made her lovelier here, it seems.
I see white ships that crowd her strands,
For mine are all the dead men's dreams.

The Breadline
(1916)
Muriel Brandt
(1909–1981)

IN A CAFE

Francis Ledwidge

Kiss the maid and pass her round,
Lips like hers were made for many.
Our loves are far from us tonight,
But these red lips are sweet as any.

Let no empty glass be seen
Aloof from our good table's sparkle,
At the acme of our cheer
Here are francs to keep the circle.

They are far who miss us most —
Sip and kiss — how well we love them,
Battling through the world to keep
Their hearts at peace, their God above them.

The Soldiers' Buffet, Charing Cross Station (1918)
Alfred Hayward (1875–1971)

An Irish Airman Foresees his Death

W. B. Yeats

I know that I shall meet my fate
Somewhere among the clouds above;
Those that I fight I do not hate,
Those that I guard I do not love;
My country is Kiltartan Cross,
My countrymen Kiltartan's poor,
No likely end could bring them loss
Or leave them happier than before.
Nor law, nor duty bade me fight,
Nor public men, nor cheering crowds,
A lonely impulse of delight
Drove to this tumult in the clouds;
I balanced all, brought all to mind,
The years to come seemed waste of breath,
A waste of breath the years behind
In balance with this life, this death.

The NCO Pilot, RFC
(Flight Sergeant W.G. Bennett), (c.1917)
William Orpen (1878–1931)

ON BEING ASKED FOR A WAR POEM

W. B. Yeats

I think it better that in times like these

A poet's mouth be silent, for in truth

We have no gift to set a statesman right;

He has had enough of meddling who can please

A young girl in the indolence of her youth,

Or an old man upon a winter's night.

The Artist's Own Dug-out on the
Albert-Braye Roadside (1916)
William Thurston Topham (1888–1966)

SIXTEEN DEAD MEN

W. B. Yeats

O but we talked at large before
The sixteen men were shot,
But who can talk of give and take,
What should be and what not
While those dead men are loitering there
To stir the boiling pot?

You say that we should still the land
Till Germany's overcome;
But who is there to argue that
Now Pearse is deaf and dumb?
And is their logic to outweigh
MacDonagh's bony thumb?

How could you dream they'd listen
That have an ear alone
For those new comrades they have found,
Lord Edward and Wolfe Tone,
Or meddle with our give and take
That converse bone to bone?

Birth of the Irish Republic
Walter Paget (1863–1935)

REPRISALS

W. B. Yeats

Some nineteen German planes, they say,
You had brought down before you died.
We called it a good death. Today
Can ghost or man be satisfied?
Although your last exciting year
Outweighed all other years, you said,
Though battle joy may be so dear
A memory, even to the dead,
It chases other thought away,
Yet rise from your Italian tomb,
Flit to Kiltartan Cross and stay
Till certain second thoughts have come
Upon the cause you served, that we
Imagined such a fine affair:
Half-drunk or whole-mad soldiery
Are murdering your tenants there.
Men that revere your father yet
Are shot at on the open plain.
Where may new-married women sit
And suckle children now? Armed men
May murder them in passing by
Nor law nor parliament take heed.
Then close your ears with dust and lie
Among the other cheated dead.

Sketch for 'Minesweepers and Seaplanes' (1917–19)
Arthur Lismer (1885–1969)

EASTER 1916

W. B. Yeats

I have met them at close of day
Coming with vivid faces
From counter or desk among grey
Eighteenth-century houses.
I have passed with a nod of the head
Or polite meaningless words,
Or have lingered awhile and said
Polite meaningless words,
And thought before I had done
Of a mocking tale or a gibe
To please a companion
Around the fire at the club,
Being certain that they and I
But lived where motley is worn:
All changed, changed utterly:
A terrible beauty is born.

That woman's days were spent
In ignorant good-will,
Her nights in argument
Until her voice grew shrill.
What voice more sweet than hers
When, young and beautiful,
She rode to harriers?
This man had kept a school
And rode our wingéd horse;
This other his helper and friend
Was coming into his force;
He might have won fame in the end,
So sensitive his nature seemed,
So daring and sweet his thought.
This other man I had dreamed
A drunken, vainglorious lout.
He had done most bitter wrong
To some who are near my heart,
Yet I number him in the song;
He, too, has resigned his part
In the casual comedy;
He, too, has been changed in his turn,
Transformed utterly:
A terrible beauty is born.

The Wingéd Horse
George 'AE' Russell (1867–1935)

Hearts with one purpose alone
Through summer and winter seem
Enchanted to a stone
To trouble the living stream.
The horse that comes from the road.
The rider, the birds that range
From cloud to tumbling cloud,
Minute by minute they change;
A shadow of cloud on the stream
Changes minute by minute;
A horse-hoof slides on the brim,
And a horse plashes within it;
The long-legged moor-hens dive,
And hens to moor-cocks call;
Minute by minute they live:
The stone's in the midst of all.

Too long a sacrifice
Can make a stone of the heart.
O when may it suffice?
That is Heaven's part, our part
To murmur name upon name,
As a mother names her child
When sleep at last has come
On limbs that had run wild.
What is it but nightfall?
No, no, not night but death;
Was it needless death after all?
For England may keep faith
For all that is done and said.
We know their dream; enough
To know they dreamed and are dead;
And what if excess of love
Bewildered them till they died?
I write it out in a verse —
MacDonagh and MacBride
And Connolly and Pearse
Now and in time to be,
Wherever green is worn,
Are changed, changed utterly:
A terrible beauty is born.

NINETEEN SIXTEEN, OR THE TERRIBLE BEAUTY

John Hewitt

Once, as a boy of nine, he heard his teacher,
Back from his interrupted holiday,
A red-faced, white-haired man, repeating wildly
All he had seen of Dublin's rash affray:

'The abandoned motor cars, the carcasses
Of army horses littering the street … '
No more remains of all he must have told them
Of that remote, ambiguous defeat.

It took those decades crammed with guns and ballads
To sanctify the names which star that myth;
And, to this day, the fierce infection pulses
In the hot blood of half our ghetto-youth.

Yet, sitting there, that long-remembered morning,
He caught no hint he'd cast an aging eye
On angled rifles, parcels left in doorways,
Or unattended cars he'd sidled by.

*British Soldiers
in Dublin
(1916)*
L.L. Davidson
(1893–1954)

TO MY DAUGHTER BETTY, THE GIFT OF GOD

Thomas Kettle

In wiser days, my darling rosebud, blown
To beauty proud as was your mother's prime,
In that desired, delayed, incredible time,
You'll ask why I abandoned you, my own,
And the dear heart that was your baby throne,
To dice with death. And oh! they'll give you rhyme
And reason: some will call the thing sublime,
And some decry it in a knowing tone.
So here, while the mad guns curse overhead,
And tired men sigh with mud for couch and floor,
Know that we fools, now with the foolish dead,
Died not for flag, nor King, nor Emperor, —
But for a dream, born in a herdsman's shed,
And for the secret Scripture of the poor.

Nurse, Wounded Soldier and Child (1915)
William Hatherell (1855–1928)

TO THE FALLEN IRISH SOLDIERS

Lord Dunsany

Since they have grudged you space in Merrion Square,
 And any monument of stone or brass,
 And you yourselves are powerless, alas,
And your own countrymen seem not to care;
Let then these words of mine drift down the air,
 Lest the world think that it has come to pass
 That *all* in Ireland treat as common grass
The soil that wraps her heroes slumbering there.

Sleep on, forgot a few more years, and then
 The ages, that I prophesy, shall see
Due honours paid to you by juster men,
 You standing foremost in our history,
Your story filling all our land with wonder,
Your names, and regiments' names,
    like distant thunder.

Etaples: British Military Cemetery
Olive Mudie-Cooke (1890–1953)

FOR ENGLAND

James Drummond Burns

The bugles of England were blowing o'er the sea,
As they had called a thousand years, calling now to me;
They woke me from dreaming in the dawning of the day,
The bugles of England — and how could I stay?

The banners of England, unfurled across the sea,
Floating out upon the wind, were beckoning to me:
Storm-rent and battle-torn, smoke-stained and grey,
The banners of England — and how cold I stay?

O England, I heard the cry of those that died for thee,
Sounding like an organ-voice across the winter sea:
They lived and died for England, and gladly went their way,
England, O England — how could *I* stay?

View of Trafalgar Square, London (1911)
Albert Henry Fullwood (1864–1930)

SWINGING THE LEAD

Banjo Patterson

Said the soldier to the Surgeon, 'I've got noises in me head
And a kind o' filled up feeling after every time I'm fed;
I can sleep all night on picket, but I can't sleep in my bed.'
    And the Surgeon said,
    'That's Lead!'

Said the soldier to the Surgeon, 'Do you think they'll
      send me back?
For I really ain't adapted to be carrying a pack
Though I've humped a case of whisky half a mile
      upon my back.'
    And the Surgeon said,
    'That's Lead!'

On the Way (c.*1918–19*)
Frank Crozier (1883–1948)

'And my legs have swelled up cruel, I can hardly walk at all,
But when the Taubes come over you should see me start to crawl;
When we're sprinting for the dugout, I can easy beat 'em all.'
    And the Surgeon said,
    'That's Lead!'

So they sent him to the trenches where he landed safe and sound,
And he drew his ammunition, just about two fifty round:
'Oh Sergeant, what's this heavy stuff I've got to hump around?'
    And the Sergeant said,
    'That's Lead!'

WHY?

Frank Westbrook

Why did I go to the wars? 'Dunno.'
No doubt is was Destiny forced me to go,
I had dashed little knowledge of national things
Pertaining to treaties and statutes and kings;
A hazy idea that a 'ell of a scrap
Was twisting and changing the tints on a map;
Grim tellings of slaughter and terrible shame,
And capping them all was Germany's name;
Of fates worse than death for a mother and maid,
Perhaps through it all I was somewhat afraid
When remembering those who are dearer to me
Than my life. And yes, there may be
In the thoughts of their honour an impelling spur
To make things quite sure for my mother and Her.
Perhaps 'twas some writer or speaker I'd heard,
The blood of my ancestors wakened and stirred,
And flung to my brain an appeal to my breed.
Mayhap I followed some other chap's lead.
Or was it the natural love of a scrap
Some sort of daredevil wakes in a chap,
That challenges death for a jest or a taunt,
The sheer joy of living that nothing will daunt?
I dunno, but I've fought and I've been through
    the mill.
What made me a soldier's a mystery still;

But home's not a home if it's not worth a fight —
All things put together I know I've done right.
Through danger and dark days and death I am here,
I'm not learned or clever, but one thing is clear,
I've a lot to be lost and dern little to gain,
But if things were reversed I'd just do it again;
For I know (for I've seen) that war is just hell,
Where death lurks with vermin and noise and
    foul smell,
But all things considered I'd go out once more,
Though I'll never know rightly what takes me to war.

At the Alert, Gas Zone (c.1918)
George Edmund Butler (1872–1936)

DAWN

Frank Westbrook

Before the Anzac landing, April 25th, 1915

The plash of the salt waves awash phosphorescent,
The outlines of hills grim and mystic grey,
The hush of the dawn ere the night curtain vanish
And morn brings the light of the flame-laden day.

The wave-bitten stretch of the grey sandy beaches,
The beaches of Anzac, the foreshores of death,
The blood of a thousand of braves soon to bleach them,
The foretaste of hell in the shells fiery breath.

Dark looming hills whether death lurks behind them,
Or whether life waits me with garlands of fame;
How can I banish the scenes of remembrance,
The dear tender thoughts of a much-cherished name?

Duty and danger call me from darkness,
The hour of my baptism fiery draws nigh;
I wonder and dream whether destiny waits me
With kisses of welcome or one brief good-bye.

Memory sings softly and croons of Australia,
Songs of my home in the Southern sea set,
Home and remembrance, the land of my fathers,
Scenes loved and lost to me, can I forget?

Flame of the wattle, the fire of the forest,
The scent of the woodbine and songs of the birds,
Incense of blossom from trees all a-flower,
The tinkle of bells from the wandering herds.

Carols of magpies when dawn is a-quiver,
The outlines of trees gaunt and ring-barked and dead,
Flash of the waratah blooming in glory,
The click of the parakeets' flight overhead.

Glimpse of the waterfowl feeding and playing
Over the face of the sleeping lagoon,
Glint of the beams opalescent and gleaming,
Silver shafts hurled from the young crescent moon.

One little home in the midst of the fallow,
The grass stringing green to the wooing of spring,
The green of the lucerne, the fruit trees in blossom,
My home way down under — how memories cling.

Ah, whether I perish or whether I follow
The scenes of the chapter of blood to the last,
My soul will dwell eager to time without ending
On dearly loved days that are banished and past.

And now I make ready for death or his master,

This though as the moments in flight hurry by —

If I live, 'tis my privilege all for my country,

For Australia to live, for Australia to die.

The Landing at Anzac (1915)
Charles Dixon (1872–1934)

ARMAGEDDON

Leon Gellert

The world rolls wet with blood,
   And the skinny hand of Death
      Gropes at the beating heart.
The salt tears well, and flood
   With strife the beating breath,
      And nations sway and part.
The scythe of Time runs red,
   Red with the bleeding year.
      Sound is but a knell,
And Sleep has a scarlet bed.
   Dreams are wet with Fear,
      And Honour sits in Hell.

An Advanced Dressing Station in France (1918)
Henry Tonks (1862–1937)

THE LAST TO LEAVE

Leon Gellert

The guns were silent, and the silent hills
    Had bowed their grasses to a gentle breeze.
I gazed upon the vales and on the rills,
    And whispered, 'What of these?' and
      'What of these?'
'These long-forgotten dead with sunken graves,
    Some crossless, with unwritten memories;
Their only mourners are the moaning waves;
    Their only minstrels are the singing trees.'

And thus I mused and sorrowed wistfully.
    I watched the place where they had scaled the height,
The height whereon they bled so bitterly
    Throughout each day and through each
      blistered night.
I sat there long, and listened — all things listened too.
    I heard the epics of a thousand trees;
A thousand waves I heard, and then I knew
    The waves were very old, the trees were wise:
The dead would be remembered evermore —
    The valiant dead that gazed upon the skies,
And slept in great battalions by the shore.

The Rearguard (The Spirit of Anzac) (1918)
Will Longstaff (1879–1953)

THE HUSBAND

Leon Gellert

Yes, I have slain, and taken moving life
    From bodies. Yea! And laughed upon the taking;
And, having slain, have whetted still the knife
    For more and more, and heeded not the making
Of things that I was killing. Such 'twas then!
    But now the thirst so hideous has left me.
I live within a coolness, among calm men,
    And yet am strange. A something has bereft me
Of a seeing, and strangely love returns;
    And old desires half-known, and hanging sorrows.
I seem agaze with wonder. Memory burns.
    I see a thousand vague and sad tomorrows.
None sees my sadness. No one understands
    How I must touch her hair with bloody hands.

The Homecoming from Gallipoli (1916)
Walter Armiger Bowring (1874–1931)

ACCEPTANCE

Leon Gellert

Beside the doors of a keen-lighted hall
    I paused, and quite by chance
        I noticed Love
Smiling and tall;
    And then I heard the whirling dance,
        And saw the dismal skies above.

She called to me to know her yet again,
    And know her pale sad friend,
        Solemn with tears;
Her friend was Pain.
    I moved away, but in the end
        Returned, fearing the empty years.

And I, who thought to scoff, and had so planned,
    I took Love's fevered arm,
        And felt Pain's breath.
I took Love's hand,
    And kissed its shining palm,
        And saw beyond the silent face of Death.

Stretcher Bearing in Difficulties (1919–1920)
Gilbert Rogers
(*c*.1885–1940)

THE TRENCHES

Frederick Manning

Endless lanes sunken in the clay,

Bays, and traverses, fringed with wasted herbage,

Seed-pods of blue scabious, and some lingering blooms;

And the sky, seen as from a well,

Brilliant with frosty stars.

We stumble, cursing, on the slippery duckboards.

Goaded like the damned by some invisible wrath,

A will stronger than weariness,

    stronger than animal fear,

Implacable and monotonous.

Here a shaft, slanting, and below

A dusty and flickering light from one

    feeble candle

And prone figures sleeping uneasily,

Murmuring,

And men who cannot sleep,

With faces impassive as masks,

Bright, feverish eyes, and drawn lips,

Sad, pitiless, terrible faces,

Each an incarnate curse.

Australian Infantry Attack in Polygon Wood (1919)
Fred Leist (1878–1945)

Here in a bay, a helmeted sentry
Silent and motionless, watching while two sleep,
And he sees before him
With indifferent eyes the blasted and torn land
Peopled with stiff prone forms, stupidly rigid,
As tho' they had not been men.

Dead are the lips where love laughed or sang,
The hands of youth eager to lay hold of life,
Eyes that have laughed to eyes,

And these were begotten
Of love, and lived lightly, and burnt
With the lust of a man's first strength:
   ere they were rent,
Almost unawares, savagely; and strewn
In bloody fragments, to be the carrion
Of rats and crows.

And the sentry moves not, searching
Night for menace with weary eyes.

The Charge of the 3rd Light Horse Brigade at the Nek, August 7th, 1915 (1916)
George Lambert (1873–1930)

GROTESQUE

Frederick Manning

These are the damned circles Dante trod,

Terrible in hopelessness,

But even skulls have their humour,

An eyeless and sardonic mockery:

And we,

Sitting with streaming eyes in the acrid smoke,

That murks our foul, damp billet,

Chant bitterly, with raucous voices

As a choir of frogs

In hideous irony, our patriotic songs.

Thiepval (1917)
William Orpen (1878–1931)

THE GUNS

Frederick Manning

Menace, hidden, but pulsing in the air of night:

Then a throbbing thunder, split and seared

With the scarlet flashes of innumerable shells,

And against it, suddenly, a shell, closer;

A purr that changes to a whine

Like a beast of prey that has missed its kill,

And again, closer.

But even in the thunder of the guns

There is a silence: and the soul groweth still.

Yea, it is cloaked in stillness:

And it is not fear.

But the torn and screaming air

Trembles under the onset of warring angels

With terrible and beautiful faces;

And the soul is stilled, knowing these awful shapes,

That burden the night with oppression,

To be but the creatures of its own lusts.

Third Ypres, July 31st, 1917;
Taking the Guns Through (1919)
H. Septimus Power (1878–1951)

THE SUPREMER SACRIFICE

Furnley Maurice (Frank Wilmot)

Close now the door; shut down the light:
    Yet can these walls my wrath provoke,
While on the altar of my Right
    My brain turns into smoke?

Close now the door, and lock the chain,
    Men have me judged, and I am glad:
I shall not cry out in my pain,
    I will go slowly mad.

Some drink the dregs of duty's cup,
    Some die, or dare their marvels through,
But I will give my reason up
    For things that I hold true.

The known is merged in the unknown,
    The serpent nestles to the dove,
And I lay all God's beauty down
    For the great God I love.

The fragrant branches wet with rain,
    The babes and bushes by the door,
The dreams that wrack my mortal brain
    Shall trouble me no more.

But I will sit, with a mild stare,
    And count the rain-drips one by one;
I shall not know the sun is there
    When next I see the sun.

*In the introduction to this poem when it was first published,
the author notes, 'In the prisons of England many
conscientious objectors have gone gradually insane.'*

*Soldat im Irrenhaus
(Soldier in the Madhouse) (1918)*
Conrad Felixmüller (1897–1977)

To God: from the Warring Nations

Furnley Maurice (Frank Wilmot)

I

We have been dead, our shroud enfolds the sea,
   Honour's a rag tossed out for winds to rend,
And Virtue is most shamed, and Lust goes free,
   While trembling Wisdom vainly seeks a friend.
Our heroes lost in trenches or the wave
   Are dust or rag, but no more dead than we,
Consigning to this universal grave
   All that is known of trust and charity.

For we assigned ourselves the frightful task
   Of healing tender wounds with filthy hands;
O God, look not into our souls, nor ask
   Defence of our loose scorn of Love's demands,
But help us that we consecrate to Thee
The remnant of our soiled humanity.

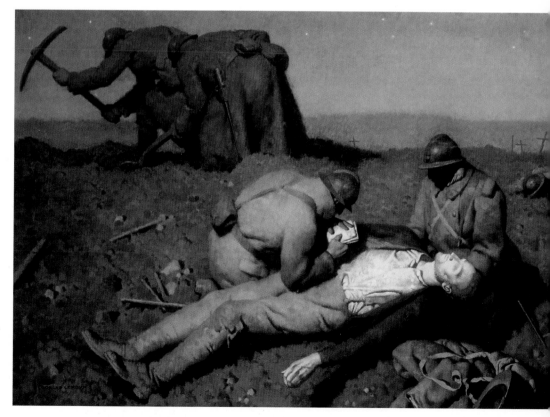

*Aux Eparges, Soldats Enterrant
leurs Camarades
au Clair de Lune (1915)*
Georges Paul Leroux (1877–1957)

II

We pray for pity, Lord, not justice, we,
    Being but mortal, offer mortal tears,
For justice would mean further cruelty,
    And we have had enough inhuman years.
Guard our repute! We have grown gross and mean,
    Who hoped to tell the future something clean!
We come, debauched, hoping and hoping not,
    Drunken with blood, burdened with all distress,
Craving for pity, Lord, who have forgot
    The name and manner of sweet gentleness.
We, being mortal, love may come again;
    Hold back severity — we are but men.
Ah! Pity, Lord! Can all indulge find
    Hope in the devious, devil-ways to Peace,
Of shamefaced, shuddering remnants of mankind
    All murdering, none brave enough to cease?
Redeem us by Thy hope lest Thy disgust
    Makes future empires violate our dust.

III

We've smashed the tablets and the songs, forsworn
    The passionate sweet pity that once reigned
Imperial; must constant fear suborn
    The hearts that guilt and grossness have so stained?
Could we be as we were ere battle came,
We would not talk of guile or separate blame.
Search not our records for the first dark ruse,
    Let the past go, sin is an old affair;
We plead for pity, Lord, not for our dues,
    We, being sinners all, must share and share.
Let us, all sinners, and all stained with blood,
    Weary with bitter consciences and lies,
Assemble in a sinners' brotherhood
    And pour out tears from our repentant eyes,
Tears for such wrongs that only tears repair.

Blood and Iron (1916)
Charles Ernest Butler (1864–1933)

IV

Ours is no cry of creed, O Lord, or race,
    But all the men the battles leave to live,
Cry from the abject pit of their disgrace,
    Implore their pitying Father to forgive.
So help them that they consecrate to Thee
    The remnant of their poor humanity.
Riot, destruction, lust, all these prevailed,
    Reason and quiet grappled, sank, and died.
Our soldiers, dreaming of home gardens, failed,
    Seeing their final dawn in the red tide.
From home's enduring husbandries beguiled,
    Hope rode in gladness from his ivied tower.
The sun was gold upon his shining dress,
    But where romance and gallantry might flower
The fight showed only blood and beastliness,
    And all the fanes of all the gods defiled.
This thing we might forget and no more see
    If Thou wouldst lay this spectre memory.

SUFFER AND FOLLOW ON

Mary Gilmore

Suffer and follow on!
That's the motto to learn;
That's the pay in the end to earn;
That's the lesson when all is gone,
And the darkest hour is come!

Suffer and follow on!
The Bugle sounds in the street
Where echoed the marching feet
Of Henri, Hans, or Albert and John,
For the call to each has come!

Suffer and follow on!
O women with breaking hearts
For lover and husband, brother and son,
What is to do when the last hour parts
But suffer and follow on!

Doughboys First
Frank Schoonover (1877–1972)

WAR
Mary Gilmore

Out in the dust he lies;
Flies in his mouth,
Ants in his eyes …

I stood at the door
Where he went out;
Full-grown man,
Ruddy and stout;

I heard the march
Of the trampling feet,
Slow and steady
Come down the street;

The beat of the drum
Was clods on the heart,
For all that the regiment
Looked so smart!

I heard the crackle
Of hasty cheers
Run like the breaking
Of unshed tears,

And just for a moment,
As he went by,
I had sight of his face,
And the flash of his eye.

He died a hero's death,
They said,
When they came to tell me
My boy was dead;

But out in the street
A dead dog lies;
Flies in his mouth,
Ants in his eyes.

A Roadside Cemetery near Neuve Eglise (1917)
George Edmund Butler (1872–1936)

THE MEASURE

Mary Gilmore

Must the young blood for ever flow?
Shall the wide wounds no closing know?
Is hate the only lantern of the stars,
And honour bastard but to scars?
And yet, the equal sun looks down
On kingly head and broken clown,
And sees, not friend and foe, but man and man,
As when these years began.

These are the days of all men's tears —
Tears like the endless drop that wears
The rock, and rusts the steel, and frets the bones
Of dead men lying under stones;
And, yet, the stars look on the earth
As in the hour of Christ His birth,
And see, not friend and foe, but man and man,
As when these years began.

Weeds on the garden pathways grow
Where the swift feet were wont to go;
Closed are the doors that stood so wide —
The white beds empty, side by side.
But in the woman-breast the milk
Tides under hodden grey and silk,
Knowing nor friend nor foe, but man's child, man,
As when these years began.

O Woman, mother of the sons of earth,
Thou holdst one measure of our worth:
A child's mouth on thy nippled breast;
A child's head on thine arm to rest!
There knowest thou, not friend or foe, but man,
As when these years began.

The Harvest (1918)
William Orpen (1878–1931)

WHO BEING DEAD ...

Vance Palmer

Mourn for the myriad eyes that death has bound
In endless night: not those for whom the sun
Grew dark with anguish ere the day was done,
Darkened till in their separate hearts they found
Pity and terror, seeing a figure crowned
With thorns, and feeling foe and comrade one,
One in that web of suffering blindly spun
As in the common haven underground:

But those who watched the evil tempest pass
And saw not evil; drowning with trivial hum
The small voice speaking in the thunder's quake,
Who watched their kindred flesh consumed like grass
And being deaf and blind remained not dumb —
Those are the dead no trump shall ever wake.

Menin Gate at Midnight (The Ghosts of Menin Gate)
Will Longstaff (1879–1953)

ROMANCE

Vance Palmer

The sunless days drag on with leaden feet,
Life moves to boasts and taunts and waving flags,
And every noble word is worn to rags
By sleek belligerents mouthing in the street,
Youth herds in camp and trench, the iron sleet
Hemming it round, crushing it in mire,
While old men feast on battles by the fire,
And hucksters raise the price of bread and meat.

Yet when our world is faded like a breath
Our children's children shall lament the dearth
Of wonder in the peace that folds them then,
And turn from trees, and flowers, and living men
To dream upon our days of war and death,
When heroes, tall and marvellous, walked the earth!

A Mother of France (c.1916)
Hilda Rix Nicholas (1884–1961)

THE FARMER REMEMBERS THE SOMME

Vance Palmer

Will they never fade or pass!
The mud, and the misty figures endlessly coming
In file through the foul morass,
And the grey flood-water lipping the reeds and grass,
And the steel wings drumming.

The hills are bright in the sun:
There's nothing changed or marred in the
　well-known places;
When work for the day is done
There's talk, and quiet laughter, and gleams of fun
On the old folks' faces.

I have returned to these:
The farm, and the kindly Bush, and the young
　calves lowing;
But all that my mind sees
Is a quaking bog in a mist — stark, snapped trees,
And the dark Somme flowing.

Butte de Polygon
(c.1918)
George Edmund Butler
(1872–1936)

THE HARVEST

Vance Palmer

The fruitful fields of Flanders
With alien blood were sown,
A thousand thousand fighting men
Have made her soil their own.

Since first by bastioned gateways
She barred her foe's advance,
Her smoking farms and flaming towns
Have lit the road to France.

And here, where all is virgin,
Her plight the brown plains know;
The axe and plough are left to rust,
That Flemish corn may grow.

Here where no trampling horsemen
Have spoiled the standing wheat,
The wide fields give their living bread
That Flemish mouths may eat.

Rich cornfields red with poppies,
Low barn and homely byre,
As in the past shall rise to hide
The blackened scars of fire.

O fruitful fields of Flanders!
Prove not the harvest vain!
The finest hands in all the world
Have helped to sow the grain.

*8th August, 1918
(1918)*
Will Longstaff
(1879–1953)

CANADA'S ANSWER

Elspeth Honeyman

Hear, O Mother of Nations, in the battle of Right and Wrong,

The voice of your youngest nation, chanting her battle-song:

Blood of your best you gave us, gave it that we might live.

Blood of our best we offer, the best of our youth we give.

The price of a nation's manhood we offer to pay the debt —

Did you dream, O Mother of Nations, that Canada could forget?

The price of a nation's manhood — we have counted the bitter cost,

(For whom can we call the victor, if the battle be won or lost?)

We pay, and we pay it gladly — ours is the Empire's need —

And a broken word has never yet found place in Britain's creed.

And when on the side of Justice, Victory takes her stand,

And a pallid peace is brooding over a broken land,

We shall count the cost but little,
    glad of the chance to pay

For a stronger chain of Empire,
    and the dawn of a better day.

Go forth, O Mother of Nations,
    to the battle of Right and Wrong,

In the strength of your young Dominions,
    to the sound of their battle-song.

Canada's Answer (c.1918)
Norman Wilkinson (1878–1971)

CANADA TO ENGLAND

Marjorie Pickthall

Great names of thy great captains gone before
    Beat with our blood who have that blood of thee:
    Raleigh and Grenville, Wolfe, and all the free
Fine souls who dared to front a world in war.
Such only may outreach the envious years
    Where feebler crowns and fainter stars remove,
    Nurtured in one remembrance and one love
Too high for passion and too stern for tears.

O little isle our fathers held for home,
    Not, not alone thy standards and thy hosts
      Lead where thy sons shall follow, Mother Land:
Quick as the north wind, ardent as the foam,
    Behold, behold the invulnerable ghosts
      Of all past greatnesses about thee stand.

War in the Air (1918)
C.R.W. Nevinson (1889–1946)

THE RECRUIT

Isabel Ecclestone Mackay

His mother bids him go without a tear;
   His sweetheart walks beside him, proudly gay,
'No coward have I loved,' her clear eyes say —
   The band blares out and all the townsfolk cheer.

Yet in his heart he thinks: 'I am afraid!
   I am afraid of Fear — how can I tell
If in the ordeal 'twill go ill or well?
   How can man tell how bravely man is made?'

Steady he waits, obeying brisk command,
   Head up, chin firm, and every muscle steeled, —
Thinking: 'I shot a rabbit in a field
   And sickened at its blood upon my hand.'

The sky is blue and little winds blow free,
   He catches up his comrades' marching-song;
Their bayonets glitter as they sweep along,
   ('How ghastly a *red* bayonet must be!')

How the folk stare! His comrade on the right
   Whispers a joke — is gay and debonair,
Sure of himself and quite at odds with care; —
   But does he, too, turn restlessly at night?

From each familiar scene his inner eye
   Turns to far fields by Titans rent and torn;
For in that struggle must his soul be born,
   To look upon itself and live — or die!

Landing of the First Canadian Division at Saint-Nazaire (c.1918)
Edgar Bundy
(1862–1922)

RENOUNCEMENT

John Daniel Logan

Kiss me good-bye! —

    And think not dear, I love thee less

    In that I haste from thy soft charms

    At war's reverberant alarms.

I am in bond to other faithfulness:

    My country calls me — I must go

    To foil my country's direst foe

    On far-off fields incarnadin'd.

    But thy too tender love is blind

    With fear and cannot see

If that I give myself, I also, dear, give thee.

Kiss me good-bye! —

    And let thine eyes be eloquent

    Of constant love while I am gone;

    And this will be my benison

    Midst scenes where death is imminent.

Nay, dear, give me your lips — and have no dread. —

    But should I fall think me not dead:

    Although I yield my mortal breath,

    We'll be inseperable in death.

    For this must ever be —

If that I give myself, I also, dear, give thee.

Return to the Front
Richard Jack (1866–1952)

A Kiss

Bernard Freeman Trotter

She kissed me when she said good-bye —
  A child's kiss, neither bold nor shy.

We had met but a few short summer hours;
  Talked of the sun, the wind, the flowers,

Sports and people; had rambled through
  A casual catchy song or two,

And walked with arms linked to the car
  By the light of a single misty star.

(It was war-time, you see, and the streets were dark
  Lest the ravishing Hun should find a mark.)

And so we turned to say good-bye;
  But somehow or other, I don't know why, —

Perhaps 'twas the feel of the khaki coat
  (She'd a brother in Flanders then) that smote

Her heart with a sudden tenderness
  Which issued in that swift caress —

Somehow, to her, at any rate
  A mere hand-clasp seemed inadequate;

And so she lifted her dewy face
  And kissed me — but without a trace

Of passion, — and we said good-bye …
  A child's kiss, … neither bold nor shy.

My friend, I like you — it seemed to say —
  Here's to our meeting again some day!
    Some happier day …
  Good-bye.

Changing Billets, Picardy (1918)
William Orpen (1878–1931)

THREE CANADIAN SOLDIERS' SONGS

WE ARE SAM HUGHES' ARMY

We are Sam Hughes' Army
No bloody good are we.
We cannot work, we cannot fight,
And why the hell should we?
And when we get to Berlin,
The Kaiser he will say,
'Hoch, hoch, Mein Gott,
What a bloody rummy lot
Is Sam Hughes' Army!

KISS ME GOODNIGHT, SERGEANT MAJOR

Kiss me goodnight, Sergeant-Major,
Tuck me in my little wooden bed.
We all love you, Sergeant-Major,
When we hear you bawling, 'Show a leg!'

Don't forget to wake me in the morning,
And bring around a nice hot cup of tea.
Kiss me goodnight, Sergeant-Major,
Sergeant-Major be a mother to me!

OH, WE ARE THE BOYS

Oh, we are the boys from the mountains
    and the prairie,
We are Canucks, you see.
We come from the East and we come
    from the West
To fight for the land of the free.
And now we're here with the rest of
    Britain's sons
And we don't give a damn for the Kaiser
    and his Huns.
We are the Canucks, you see.

Canadian Observation Post (1920)
Colin Unwin Gill (1892–1940)

I Didn't Raise My Boy to be a Soldier

Alfred Bryan

Ten million soldiers to the war have gone
Who may never return again,
Ten million mothers' hearts must break
For the ones who died in vain.
Head bowed down in sorrow
In her lonely years,
I heard a mother murmur thro' her tears:

I didn't raise my boy to be a soldier,
I brought him up to be my pride and joy.
Who dares to put a musket on his shoulder,
To shoot some other mother's darling boy?

Let nations arbitrate their future troubles,
It's time to lay the sword and gun away,
There'd be no war today,
If mothers all would say,
I didn't raise my boy to be a soldier.

What victory can cheer a mother's heart
When she looks at her blighted home?
What victory can bring her back,
All she cared to call her own?
Let each mother answer
In the years to be,
'Remember that my boy belongs to me!'

For What? (c.1918)
Frederick H. Varley (1881–1969)

THE SOLDIER

Frank Prewett

My years I counted twenty-one
Mostly at tail of plough:
The furrow that I drove is done,
To sleep in furrow now.

I leapt from living to the dead
A bullet was my bane
It split this nutshell rind of head,
This kernel of a brain.

A lad to life has paid his debts
Who bests and kills his foe,
And man upon his sweethearts gets,
To reap as well as sow.

But I shall take no son by hand,
No grey beard bravo be:
My ghost is tethered in the sand
Afar from my degree.

Canadian Sentry, Moonlight, Neuville-Vitesse (1918)
Alfred Bastien (1873–1955)

THE SILENT TOAST

Frederick George Scott

They stand with reverent faces,
    And their merriment give o'er,
As they drink the toast to the unseen host
    Who have fought and gone before.

It is only a passing moment
    In the midst of the feast and song,
But it grips the breath, as the wing of death
    In a vision sweeps along.

No more they see the banquet
    And the brilliant lights around;
But they charge again on the hideous plain
    When the shell-bursts rip the ground.

Or they creep at night, like panthers,
    Through the waste of No Man's Land,
Their hearts afire with a wild desire,
vAnd death on every hand.

And out of the roar and tumult,
    Or the black night loud with rain,
Some face comes back on the fiery track
    And looks in their eyes again.

And the love that is passing woman's,
    And the bonds that are forged by death,
Now grip the soul with a strange control
    And speak what no man saith.

The vision dies off in the stillness,
    Once more the tables shine,
But the eyes of all in the banquet hall
    Are lit with a light divine.

No Man's Land
Maurice Cullen (1866–1934)

A CANADIAN
Frederick George Scott

The glad and brave young heart
  Had come across the sea,
He longed to play his part
  In crushing tyranny.

The mountains and the plains
  Of his beloved land
Were wine within his veins
  And gave an iron hand.

He scorned the thought of fear,
  He murmured not at pain,
The call of God was clear,
  The path of duty plain.

Beneath the shower of lead
  Of poison and of fire,
He charged and fought and bled
  Ablaze with one desire.

O Canada, with pride
  Look up and greet the morn,
Since of thy wounded side
  Such breed of men is born.

Mud (1919)

Gilbert Rogers (*c.*1885–1940)

THE UNCONQUERED DEAD

John McCrae

Not we the conquered! Not to us the blame
   Of them that flee, of them that basely yield;
Nor ours the shout of victory, the fame
   Of them that vanquish in a stricken field.

That day of battle in the dusty heat
   We lay and heard the bullets swish and sing
Like scythes amid the over-ripened wheat,
   And we the harvest of their garnering.

Some yielded. No, not we! Not we, we swear
   By these our wounds; this trench upon the hill
Where all the shell-strewn earth is seamed and bare,
   Was ours to keep; and lo! we have it still.

We might have yielded, even we, but death
   Came for our helper; like a sudden flood
The crashing darkness fell; our painful breath
   We drew with gasps amid the choking blood.

The roar fell faint and farther off, and soon
   Sank to a foolish humming in our ears,
Like crickets in the long, hot afternoon
   Among the wheat fields of the olden years.

Before our eyes a boundless wall of red
   Shot through by sudden streaks of jagged pain!
Then a slow-gathering darkness overhead
   And rest came on us like a quiet rain.

Not we the conquered! Not to us the shame,
   Who hold our earthen ramparts, nor shall cease
To hold them ever; victors we, who came
   In that fierce moment to our honoured peace.

The Conquerors (1920)
Eric Henry Kennington (1888–1960)

IN FLANDERS FIELDS

John McCrae

In Flanders fields the poppies blow
Between the crosses, row on row,
That mark our place; and in the sky
The larks, still bravely singing, fly
Scarce heard amid the guns below.

We are the Dead. Short days ago
We lived, felt dawn, saw sunset glow,
Loved, and were loved, and now we lie
In Flanders fields.

Take up our quarrel with the foe:
To you from failing hands we throw
The torch; be yours to hold it high.
If ye break faith with us who die
We shall not sleep, though poppies grow
In Flanders fields.

Kummel Road, Flanders
Mary Riter Hamilton (1873–1954)

CONVOCATION HALL

Helena Coleman

They rose,
The honoured and the grave,
The reverend, the grey,
While one read out the names of those
Who, gallant, young and brave,
Upon the field of battle gave
Their ardent lives away.

They rose to honour Youth —
What honour could they give?
What tribute shall we lay
Who still in safety live?

Before the shrine of those who pay
The price of honour and of truth
Giving their lives away?

They rose in reverence, yea;
But those who lie
Far on the Flanders field today
Had not an answering word to say;
Their silence thundered their reply —
They gave their lives away!

*The Cemetery at Mont
St Eloi (1918)*
Herbert Hughes-Stanton
(1843–1914)

THE STRETCHER-BEARER

Robert Service

My stretcher is one scarlet stain,
And as I tries to scrape it clean,
I tell you wot — I'm sick with pain
For all I've 'eard, for all I've seen;
Around me is the 'ellish night,
And as the war's red rim I trace,
I wonder if in 'Eaven's height,
Our God don't turn away 'Is Face.

I don't care 'oose the Crime may be;
I 'olds no brief for kin or clan;
I 'ymns no 'ate: I only see
As man destroys his brother man;
I waves no flag: I only know,
As 'ere beside the dead I wait,
A million 'earts is weighed with woe,
A million 'omes is desolate.

In drippin' darkness, far and near,
All night I've sought them woeful ones.
Dawn shudders up and still I 'ear
The crimson chorus of the guns.
Look! like a ball of blood the sun
'Angs o'er the scene of wrath and wrong ...
'Quick! Stretcher-bearers on the run!'
O Prince of Peace! 'ow long, 'ow long?

An RAMC Stretcher-Bearer (1919)
Gilbert Rogers (*c.*1885–1940)

The Stretcher-Bearer Party (c.1918)
Cyril Barraud (1877–1965)

FAITH

Robert Service

Since all that is was ever bound to be;
    Since grim, eternal laws our Being bind;
    And both the riddle and the answer find,
And both the carnage and the calm decree;
Since plain within the Book of Destiny
    Is written all the journey of mankind
    Inexorably to the end; since blind
And mortal puppets playing parts are we:

Then let's have faith; good cometh out of ill;
    The power that shaped the strife shall end the strife;
Then let's bow down before the Unknown Will;
    Fight on, believing all is well with life;
Seeing within the worst of War's red rage,
The gleam, the glory of the Golden Age.

The Kensingtons at Laventie (1915)
Eric Henry Kennington
(1888–1960)

THE LARK

Robert Service

From wrath-red dawn to wrath-red dawn,
   The guns have brayed without abate;
And now the sick sun looks upon
   The bleared, blood-boltered fields of hate
As if it loathed to rise again.
   How strange the hush! Yet sudden, hark!
From yon down-trodden gold of grain,
   The leaping rapture of a lark.

A fusillade of melody,
   That sprays us from yon trench of sky;
A new amazing enemy
   We cannot silence though we try;
A battery on radiant wings,
   That from yon gap of golden fleece
Hurls at us hopes of such strange things
   As joy and home and love and peace.

Pure heart of song! Do you not know
   That we are making earth a hell?
Or is it that you try to show
   Life still is joy and all is well?
Brave little wings! Ah, not in vain
   You beat into that bit of blue:
Lo! we who pant in war's red rain
   Lift shining eyes, see Heaven too.

Poppy Land
Mildred Anne Butler (1858–1941)

THE MOURNERS

Robert Service

I look into the aching womb of night;
   I look across the mist that masks the dead;
The moon is tired and gives but little light,
    The stars have gone to bed.

The earth is sick and seems to breathe with pain;
   A lost wind whimpers in a mangled tree;
I do not see the foul, corpse-cluttered plain,
    The dead I do not see.

The slain I *would* not see ... and so I lift
   My eyes from out the shambles where they lie;
When lo! a million woman-faces drift
    Like pale leaves through the sky.

The cheeks of some are channelled deep with tears;
   But some are tearless, with wild eyes that stare
Into the shadow of the coming years
    Of fathomless despair.

And some are young, and some are very old;
   And some are rich, some poor beyond belief;
Yet all are strangely like, set in the mould
    Of everlasting grief.

They fill the vast of Heaven, face on face;
   And then I see one weeping with the rest,
Whose eyes beseech me for a moment's space ...
    Oh eyes I love the best!

Nay, I but dream. The sky is all forlorn,
   And there's the plain of battle writhing red:
God pity them, the women-folk who mourn!
    How happy are the dead!

Sacrifice (c.1918)
Charles Sims (1873–1928)

PILGRIMS

Robert Service

For oh! when the war will be over
    We'll go and we'll look for our dead;
We'll go when the bee's on the clover,
    And the plume of the poppy is red;
We'll go when the year's at its gayest,
    When meadows are laughing with flow'rs;
And there where the crosses are greyest,
    We'll seek for the cross that is ours.

For they cry to us: 'Friends, we are lonely,
    A-weary the night and the day;
But come in the blossom-time only,
    Come when our graves will be gay:
When daffodils all are a-blowing,
    And larks are a-thrilling the skies,
Oh, come with the hearts of you glowing,
    And the joy of the Spring in your eyes.

But never, oh never come sighing,
    For ours was the Splendid Release;
And oh, but 'twas joy in the dying
    To know we were winning you Peace!
So come when the valleys are sheening,
    And fledged with the promise of grain;
And here where our graves will be greening,
    Just smile and be happy again.'

And so, when the war will be over,
    We'll seek for the Wonderful One;
And maiden will look for her lover,
    And mother will look for her son;
And there will be end to our grieving,
    And gladness will gleam over loss,
As — glory beyond all believing! —
    We point … to a name on a cross.

Some Day the People will Return (1918)
Fred Varley (1881–1969)

THE SURVIVOR

Frank Prewett

What this reptile worm or snake
Creeps on its torpid scales, creeps
Winding and lengthening its wake
While God above it sleeps.

Tempest crushes it, wind assails:
On its bayonets gleam
Lightnings, yet it prevails
And filters through valley and stream.

A thousand men to make a beast
That beast more cumbered each:
Sodden and splintered to the feast,
The muddied feast of death they reach.

We are mad after thirty years,
We who live are mad in the peace.
I left my life there, kept its fears:
From the regiment is no release.

While the shells crashed we were strong,
Grenade and sniper we defied:
Now I am old, stay overlong —
For in those many men I died.

The Return to Mons (1920)
Inglis Sheldon-Williams (1870–1940)

THE LITTLE CAR
Guillaume Apollinaire

A little before midnight I left Deauville

In Rouveyre's little car

Counting the chauffeur we were three

We said farewell to a whole era

Furious giants were rising over Europe

Eagles flew from their eyrie to wait for the sun

Voracious fish ascended from abysses

Nations hurled together so they might learn to know one another

The dead trembled fearfully in their dark dwellings

Dogs barked yonder where the frontiers were

I went off carrying within me all those armies that were fighting

I felt them rise within me and where they meandered the landscape spread out

With forests happy villages in Belgium

Francorchamps where the Red Water is and the springs

Region where invasions always start

Railway arteries where those going off to die

Hailed once more brightly coloured life

Deep oceans where monsters were moving

In old shipwrecked carcasses

Unimaginable heights where man fights

Higher than the eagle glides

Man fights there against man
And suddenly falls like a shooting star

I felt within me skilful new beings
Build and even arrange a new universe
A merchant with unheard-of wealth and whose
    size was prodigious
Arranged an extraordinary showcase
In which humanity was merchandise
And giant shepherds led
Great silent flocks that nibbled words
They were barked at by all the dogs on the road

Translated by Anne Hyde Greet

The Road from Arras to Bapaume (1917)
C.R.W. Nevinson (1889–1946)

OFFERING

Nicolas Beauduin

I offer thee the life thou gavest me,
I offer thee my flesh that thou didst mould,
I offer thee, my country, my ardent soul;
Land of my birth, my blood be seed in thee.

May this, my body's fervent last oblation,
When this my sacrifice has fully bled,
Be pleasing to you, powers of salvation
Who guide the living and protect the dead.

Translated by Ian Higgins

l'Église d'Ablain-Saint-Nazaire (1915)
François Flameng (1856–1923)

VENI, SANCTE SPIRITUS!
from A SONG OF WELCOME TO THE NEW YEAR

Jean-Pierre Calloc'h

Now in the one thousand nine hundred and fourteenth year after Christ was born in the stable;

Like the Poor man's face all at once against the windows of the worldly rich at their wild dancing;

Like the three words on the wall, when Belshazzar made his great feast;

Like a moon of grief and terror, blinding each day's sun with its savage splendour,

Over every contemptible horizon of the Strumpet Europe,

The blood-face of War!

And before that terrible Star every star fell back, cast into the depths of night;

And all works ceased, until the Great Work should be wrought;

And men fixed their eyes upon fields of carnage, the place of celebration of a great Mystery, a transcendental Sacrifice,

The Mass whose celebrant is Fire, its unexampled music the gun, the Mass whose victim they call the son of man.

I sleep no more. There is a voice in the winter night, calling to me, a strange voice;

A strong voice, and harsh, a voice accustomed to command: such a voice rings agreeably in young men's ears;

(And it is no woman's voice, nor that mermaid voice that haunts the Celtic sea);

A voice that none can disobey: War, howling at the frontiers.

I will obey. Soon I shall be with my brothers, a soldier following soldiers.

Soon I shall be among the slaughter … What signs are on my brow? New year, shall I see your end?

But it is of no account! Sooner, or later, when the hour to approach the Father sounds, I shall go with gladness. Jesus shall comfort our mothers.

Be blessed, new year, even should, among your three hundred and sixty-five days, there be my last!

Be blessed! For more than one hundred years have passed over this land and known only the anger of God, but you shall witness His mercies.

You shall see banished beliefs return, the wings of victory spread again, under the beating flag of France, and our country exalted for evermore;

You shall see my Brittany free at last, and her language held in honour, as it was when her knights were alive to defend her.

New year, year of war! Be blessed, even should you bring, wrapped in the folds of your cloak, next to springtime for the world, death for me.

What is the death of one man, or one hundred, the death of one hundred thousand men, if our country only lives, if the race still lives … ?

When I die, say the prayers and bury me like my fathers, my face set towards the enemy,

And ask nothing for me of my Redeemer, except the last place in His Paradise …

I know that You will come. I know that You are near. I believe in the mystery of Grief.

'There is no birth without pain' is life's teaching to the bard. And the bard's to life:
'No pain without a birth. There is no sorrow that is barren, for such is the Law;

And has been, since Sorrow found a wedded Husband, Him whom the centuries have crucified, and crucified.'

The seed must die if it is to spring up and thrive. I see the bodies of my brethren like seeds in the earth: on their ashes wonderful fruit shall thrive …

Like a barbarian king who wraps himself in crimson before lying down to die, the year's last sun has sunk in a shroud of blood …

Tomorrow the sun shall shine upon the World!

And, like the woman in labour when she sees the face of the child born to her, when it sees the beauty of the new Day the Earth shall not remember its pain.

Translated by Ian Higgins

l'Yser (1915)
George Bertin Scott (1873–1943)

TO NORMAN LADS

Lucie Delarue-Mardrus

Splendid hedges, splendid beasts;
The fields and blossom of dreams,
The sky a coloured, mirrored feast
Bubbling down the stream

Through perfect pasture to the sea;
Hay ready for the manger —
Such is our country: keep her free,
Our country is in danger!

Do you own, or simply work, the land? —
Arise and and hurry! Now!
Stout of heart and firm of hand,
Save the fields you plough.

The foe might come by sea, to this shore;
By land, or from the skies.
Listen how your stallion cries!
To war, you must to war.

Norman lads have eyes of blue,
Let them glint and pierce.
March cheerful, though the guns be fierce,
Battalions bold and true.

Away to fight, my warrior kin,
Take the road to fame.
Tomorrow's history shall begin
With your impatient name.

Our country bids you leave your corn,
The harvest still not done!
But flowers from your fields adorn
The muzzles of your guns.

Make haste! Sing as you depart,
And you arm for carnival;
March with poems in your heart,
And war is festival.

A great tragedy is about to play.
Leave no thing to chance:
Arise, my Normandy, away
And save the soil of France!

Translated by Ian Higgins

Le Château de Suzanne (1916)
François Flameng (1856–1923)

GAMECOCKS

Edmond Adam

I come crawling out of my hole,
my black trench, where the mud
sucks us back.
Neck stretched out I crawl,
not daring raise my head,
temples hot with thudding blood.
I crawl,
and after me my men
come crawling
through the mud,
till they catch in the wire
and it screeches, and skins them
with hatchet fangs,
and clashes on their bayonets.

Rat-tat-tat … Zing! Zing!
Lie flat … Rat-tat-tat … Zing!
If only we could flatten further.
'They've seen us … They've heard us!'
Bayonet-sharp,
a shudder chills our spines …
My clenched fist clutches my revolver.
And I do just raise my head,
brow and body sweat-soaked.

But they've stopped firing.
We struggle further forward,
Crawling … Shh!!
For God's sake make less noise!
Careful with your bayonets.
You over there, come on!
Crack! … Shhwhizzz …
A flare comes climbing to its zenith
and opens out, a blinding flower
over our cringing heads.

Rat-tat-tat! … We can't be seen,
but: Rat-tat-tat-tat-tat! … and: Zing! Zing! Zing!
Boche bastards!
Then blacker night returns,
and we can find a shell-hole
and breathe again.

Ker-rack! … Ker-rack! …
This is horrible!
Zing! … Rat-tat-tat!
For God's sake, Boche bastard,
how long's it going on for,
this machine gun?
Yes, I know: you can see us crawling
towards you.

So, behind your parapet
you're pumping your mechanical pig.
Wouldn't you just love to smash us …
If you heard us scream, you savage,
wouldn't you just roar: 'Komm, Fritz!
Hör' die Französen singen!'
Rat-tat-tat! … Rat-tat-tat! …
But what have we done to you?
We're in the middle of our wire, *our* wire;
we're going to cut a way right through!
Tomorrow, when we've reached you,
and the raid's on, hell, defend yourself then,
fire then — but not tonight!
just leave us be, we've work to do.

Rat-tat! … Zing! …
All right, you brute,
go on, fire!
That's what you're there for. Fire away!
You're doing your job, like us.
Ker-rack!
We don't give a damn,
fire all you like —
you can't see us, you're firing blind
at the night we're hidden in.
Your pig's spitting in the wind.

I don't really mind, you know.
That's four years now you've been on this job
behind your parapet …
And we've been at work for four years, too,
knitting great meshes of entanglement,
then cutting fresh tracks through them, ready
to attack next day and flush you
from your trenches.

Look — your works gates
are next to mine, we're almost mates.
We've been flogging ourselves for rival firms,
each as bad as the other, perhaps —
we can't be sure!
My boss has told me yours
is a villainous, treacherous, murderous,
good-for-nothing swine!
But yours, perhaps,
has said the same of mine.

Anyhow, we're scrapping like dogs,
like gamecocks
with masters relentlessly
and furiously betting one another
and themselves into frenzy;
when it's over, one'll be ruined,
and the other no better off.

And their birds'll have slashed each other

to shreds, feathers and flesh,

and bled to death ...

Rat-tat! Rat-tat!

That'll do, old son!

You're stupider than those cocks.

Zing! ... Zing! ...

You idiot! Don't be stupid!

Rat-tat! ... Right, I've had enough!

My master's right,

you're just a brute.

Perhaps you'll kill me.

I've got children and a wife ...

Rat-tat!

Old son, you're going to pay for this.

I'll skewer you tomorrow,

  right by your Spandau!

And if you've got a wife,

that's just too bad,

and too bad for your children!

I'm a brute as well,

when I'm pushed too far.

Passage du Canal de l'Yser (1917)
François Flameng (1856–1923)

And we'll do as brave gamecocks do, when

they're thrown into the pit at one another,

and unflinchingly, heroically

and ruthlessly fight,

till they drop and die at nightfall of their wounds,

roared on and clapped by an ecstatic crowd,

for the glory, but the ruin too,

alas,

of their unpardonable masters.

Translated by Ian Higgins

from THE SOLDIER'S SOLILOQUIES

Marc de Larreguy de Civrieux

I

After the Charleroi affair
And since we waved the Marne goodbye,
I drag my carcass everywhere,
But never know the reason why.

In trench or barn I spend each day,
From fort or attic glimpse the sky,
At this war simply slog away,
But never know the reason why.

I ask, hoping to understand
This slaughter's purpose. The reply
I get is: 'For the Motherland!'
But never know the reason why.

Better for me to just keep mum
And, when it's my own turn to die,
Depart this life for kingdom come,
But never know the reason why.

Burial Party at Bellevue, near Solesmes (c.1918)
George Edmund Butler (1872–1936)

IV

The civvy says: 'How dear is Life!'
I think it's cheap, because I know
A certain cut-rate Butcher's Wife
Whose prices are absurdly low.
She is a Phrygian, red-capped,
Her chops dripping with blood fresh tapped,
Browed like a beast and harlot-eyed,
Tossing unwanted meat aside!

To the vile cattle-mart she goes,
Then straight to slaughter-house she flies
To rain her vicious cleaver-blows
On men, who gasp their anguished cries
As her huge fists above them rise!

Slicing away, she cuts and trims
Flesh from their skulls and all their limbs;
And then this putrid meat she throws
Down on a slab that's marked 'Heroes'
As bait for rats and worms and crows!

Do you still say, 'How dear is Life'
When it's dirt-cheap (that's my advice)?
Why then accept at knock-down price
That offal from the Butcher's Wife?

Come, eat! Carry the Dead Men in!
They can still serve the Living band
Who've not regarded it a sin
To have them slaughtered out of hand,
So saving their own precious skin!

O souls righteous in charity,
To salve your Consciences chant happily,
Before you settle down to eat,
A prayer, duly mild and sweet,
Addressed to the 'new Trinity'!
In chorus chant the 'Benedicite'
As you feast on humanity! ...

The sacrifice divine thus glorify
And then your absolution claim:
'For Right and Justice,' be your cry,
'And in Civilisation's name!!!'

Translated by D.D.R. Owen

MOBILISATION

Henriette Sauret

From men, wild slaves are wrought,
With hobbled limbs and ducking heads;
From women, Vulcan's skivvies, forced
To knead bronze instead of bread.

Wood, rope, leather, glass, coal —
All gone for soldiers. A spate
Of eager coin and gold
Has paid for weapons, man-created

Teeth for man to eat men. The very trees
Are mobilised and piteously deployed,
Wellsprings, hills, the air, the sea —
Today, no man or thing is unemployed.

The players weary — nothing's done by halves
And he who crosses Nature's like to starve!
We'd best destroy the gardens straight away —
Flowers and lovesome bowers have had their day!

Plough up the lawns, grub out the shrubs and trees,
Forget about providing food for bees.
Sweet lilies, roses, violets demure,
You will all make excellent manure.
Our parks we'll deck with turnip clamps and straw.

Such are the beauties of war.

Translated by Ian Higgins

Les Pommiers Coupés à Cuts (Oise) (1917)
François Flameng (1856–1923)

I Always Thought ...

Cécile Périn

I always thought that, clasped in a lover's arms,
 Being weak was heaven-sent,
And that soft surrender to a strong embrace
 Embraced with equal strength.

But now I hate — how I hate — my weakness.
 I hate these feeble wrists
That used to stroke him, smooth and sinuous
 In their bangles and bracelets,

And this lissome, living body, on a chain
 At the doors of empty dwellings,
That curls up and sleeps when cries of human pain
 And anguish fill the heavens.

Translated by Ian Higgins

Le Récit (1917)
François Flameng (1856–1923)

THE NORTH WIND ...

Cécile Périn

The north wind whistling round the doors,
Snow, filling the lanes and tracks with white.
Wartime April, April caught
And pinioned with the gale's lash,
April of the stricken light.

The women wear black veils,
The girls a grown-up dignity.
The talk is in murmurs. Night
Closes in ... Silence ... A splinter
Of hope gleams in the dark, like driftwood.

Here we sit, no one speaking now.
What do you say to a woman crying?
Here we sit, like prisoners.
Never stirring, each in her house,
We sit, and know the men are dying.

Translated by Ian Higgins

Destroyed Forest near Verdun (1916)
Adolf Erbslöh (1881–1947)

NOCTURNE

Albert-Paul Granier

The guns have fallen silent, gagged with fog,
in the winter's night that cancels space,
and a calm, full of menace
as the screech of owls over castle walls,
hangs in the many-hearted silence.

Sentries, peering out,
tense every muscle, edgily
awaiting the unexpected.

A thwack like wet cloth
sounds from the valley —
sudden muffled rifle-shots
unsure of guessed-at shadows
and the rustling emptiness.

Tonight
is like the nights in Breton legend
when hell-hag washerwomen
kneel invisible at riverside stones,
beating shrouds in the thick water.

L'offensive de l'Yser (1917)
François Flameng (1856–1923)

Translated by Ian Higgins

MARKET

Cécile Périn

Comings, goings, bustlings to and fro
   With a 'How are you, Madame?'
And 'Lovely morning!' 'Aren't things dear though!'
   'But one has to eat, Madame!'

There is a mass of peonies on the stalls,
   Piles of pink and red; peonies;
And slender women swaying home under stacks
   Of flowers. There are peonies.

And the war, of course. But so far away.
   A lovely day, you just forget.
A long way off, and no real news for days …
   — How might they all *not* forget?

Translated by Ian Higgins

The Flower Market (1916)
Victor-Gabriel Gilbert (1847–1933)

THERE IS THERE ARE

Guillaume Apollinaire

There's a ship that has sailed away with my love

There are six sausages in the sky and night coming on you'd say maggots that will hatch into stars

There's an enemy submarine with designs on my love

There are a thousand little pines shattered by the bursting shells around me

There's a foot soldier passing by who is blinded by the asphyxiating gas

There's everything we have slashed to pieces in the gutlike trenches of Nietzsche Goethe
   and Cologne

There's my longing for a letter that doesn't come

There are snapshots in my wallet of my love

There are the prisoners going by with troubled looks

There's a battery whose gun crew is busy with the guns

There's the post orderly who arrives trotting along the trail of the lonesome pine

There's a spy they say who prowls by here invisible like the horizon which he is shamelessly
   wearing and which he blends with

There is erect like a lily the portrait of my love

There is a captain waiting anxiously for messages from the TSF about the Atlantic

There are soldiers at midnight sawing planks for coffins

There are women asking for corn with great cries before a bleeding Christ in Mexico City

There's the Gulf Stream so lukewarm and so beneficial

There's a cemetery full of crosses 5 kilometers away

There are crosses everywhere on this side or that

There are Barbary figs on the cactus in Algeria

There are my love's long supple hands

There's an inkwell I made in a 15-centimeter rocket they didn't send off

There's my saddle out in the rain

There are the rivers that won't flow uphill again

There's love that gently allures me

There was a Boche prisoner carrying his machine gun on his back

There are men in the world who have never been to war

There are Hindus watching in astonishment the Western landscapes

They think sadly of their friends and wonder if they'll see them again

For we have pushed very far in this war the art of invisibility

Translated by Anne Hyde Greet

Heavy Artillery (1919)
Colin Unwin Gill (1892–1940)

IN THE DUGOUT

Guillaume Apollinaire

I project myself toward you and I think that you too project yourself toward me

A force issues from us it's a solid fire welding us together

And yet paradoxically we can't see each other

Facing me the chalk wall crumbles

Filled with fractures

Long traces of tools sleek traces that appear to be made of stearin

Edges of fractures are torn by the fellows in my room passing by

As for me tonight I have a soul that's hollow and empty

You could say in my soul someone keeps falling and finding no bottom

And there's nothing to grab onto

What keeps falling and living inside me is a crowd of ugly beings that hurt me I don't know
   where they come from

But I think they come from life from a kind of life still in the future a raw future not yet
   refined or exalted or humanised

In the huge emptiness of my soul there isn't any sun there's nothing that gives light

It's today it's tonight but it's not for always

Luckily it's just for tonight

Most days I cling to you

Most days I console myself for loneliness and all kinds of horrors

By imagining your beauty

And raising it above the ecstatic universe

Then I start wondering if I imagine it in vain

For I can't know your beauty by my senses

Or even by words

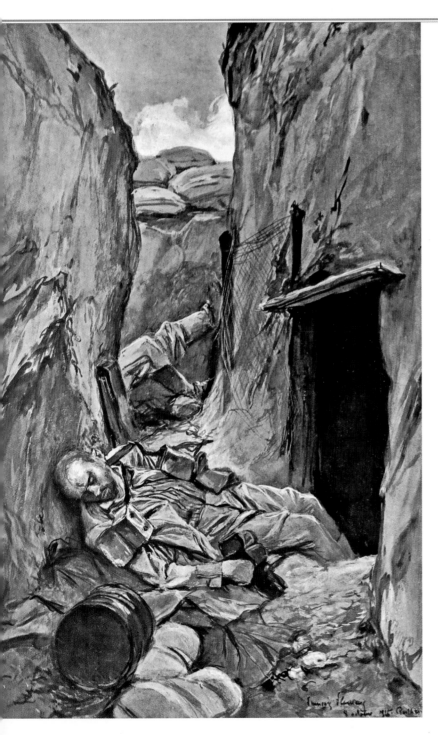

Then is my fondness for beauty also in vain
Do you really exist my love
Or are you only a being I created involuntarily
So that I might people my loneliness
Are you a goddess like those the Greeks
    instated so as to feel less weary
I worship you my delicate goddess even if you
    are only the creature of my thought

Translated by Anne Hyde Greet

Tranchée Conquise à Perthes (1915)
François Flameng (1856–1923)

WAR

Guillaume Apollinaire

Central combat sector

   Contact by sound

We're firing toward 'noises that were heard'

The young men of the class of 1915

And those electrified wires

Then don't weep for the horrors of war

Before the war we had only the surface

Of the earth and the seas

After it we'll have the depths

Subterranean and aerial space

Masters of the helm

After after

We'll assume all the joys

Of conquerors in repose

Women Games Factories Trade

Industry Agriculture Metal

Fire Crystal Speed

Voice Gaze Touch separately

And together in the touch of things from far away

From farther still

From the Beyond of this earth

Translated by Anne Hyde Greet

Notre Aviation de Guerre (1918)
François Flameng (1856–1923)

DE PROFUNDIS

Jean-Marc Bernard

The trenches, Lord, are stark and deep,
We raise our hands towards you.
The steps out of the dark are dark and steep,
Have mercy on our souls!

Exhaustion of the spirit is worse
Than of the body. On our heads
A hurricane of death and pain has burst,
Flame, iron rain and flood.

You see us ragged, caked with mud,
Haggard, disheartened, weary.
But have you seen our naked souls, O God?
Shall we confess the worst?

Peace is intangible as prayer
And every day more distant.
This quagmire where we crouch is named Despair;
Faint is the lamp of duty.

Give us some heart, some light, console
Us in this mire, this pit of Hell,
And heal the soldier's agony of soul.
Restore our resolution.

But those who suffered in the trenches' mud
And in this mud lie buried,
Clothed in their sacramental blood —
Grant them the peace they merit.

Translated by Graham Dunstan Martin

Dernière Vision (1914)
George Bertin Scott (1873–1943)

YOUNG SHADES
Anna de Noailles

Limpid Summer evening, swimming
With swallows twisting and swooping,
Tranquil landscape, horizon
Awash with sunshine, blue sky
Lit with yellow plums —
What have you done with all the faces?

The faces of the youthful dead
Dissolved in your fluidity?
The handsome dead, sprung
By the hair-fine triggers of Spring
And the switches and filaments of Summer
Up into the urgent spreading foliage
Of earth's eternity.

Nimble, scintillating sap
That Nature is built from,
What have you done with their dreams,
Lulled in your pulse, lulled in your breathing,
And fulfilled as dew
In the cold, reposing shade?

These dead are the very flesh of day,
They are the fruit, the vine, the wheat;
Their sacred bones, distilled and gathering
Through roots and stalks, now fill and consummate
The spotlessness of space.

But that sweet, terrible love
That all the universe shouts of,
The stir and jubilation of desire,
Arms opening to shuddering gasps,
The ecstasy of tears and fire,
Those high triumphant moments
That no other glory can touch,
When we are Destiny's match
And the spasms inside us
Are beating out a future —
Who shall restore all this to the countless dead?
Who shall restore it to you, poor shades,
In your numberless oneness
Pining in the skies of Summer nights?

Translated by Ian Higgins

Le Triomphateur
François Flameng (1856–1923)

TO CAM

Henriette Charasson

Only for rare, short moments do I ever understand, at last, my darling brother, that you are dead.

For me, you left months ago and I simply think you have been away too long,

And I live my life as if I were sure they are holding you there in their gloomy forests,

But I believe you will come back on the day when the bugles sound our victory.

And I wait for you, and wear no black veils, and when friends' eyes fill with pity,
I am all stubborn poise.

And they wonder that I can be so brave — but where is the bravery, when I still believe
you will come back to me,

When I believe that I shall see you walk back in one day through this old porch,
in the pale blue uniform you wore when you left, that last evening?

Together, we had walked out along the path through the peaceful fields,

And you, as you often do, had your hand on my shoulder, gentle and protective.
And we walked along, as one, in perfect step, as night fell round us.

— And that evening, perhaps, more than ever, was when we felt our love's full force.
You left with a smile, and said to us all: 'Back soon!'

— So how should I think you will never come back, when every promise you ever made
you have kept?

It would be the first time you had ever deceived me …

— And how pointless loving you would be, and how paltry my love,

If it failed to bring you back to me, back from where they say you lie amongst the dead!

No one has shown me proof that you are amongst the dead,

And I can place no reliance on their flimsy affirmations.

And I sit waiting for you, for there must always be a woman to watch the night-light,

Lest the sick man think he is alone and the soul depart the body.

Can you perhaps, if you're still alive, can you perhaps sense the still, small flame

From across the ravaged provinces that lie between us?

Sleep, my silent one, and rest; have no fear for the light, it shan't go out;

I feel I shall wait for you, month in, month out, my whole life long;

When my hair is white, I shall still be hoping to see you walk back in through this porch.

Only for rare, short moments can I ever, sometimes, understand that you are dead.

Translated by Ian Higgins

Deux Héros (1915)
George Bertin Scott (1873–1943)

By Evening's Blue-Grey Threshold ...

Gaston de Ruyter

By evening's blue-grey threshold stirs a breeze;
And all along the road the bowing trees,
Though gale and tempest have now turned to flight,
Trembled to sense it lost in the dark night:

A breath of trust, tenderly soothing pain,
Has crept about the hollows of the plain.
While raging hearts have quivered in their hate,
A breath of love prompts dreams of happier fate.

As the north wind drove the mills ceaselessly
And death too let its sombre sails turn free,
Frail, lissom women, stooping with bowed head,
Closed for all time the eyelids of the dead.

Ah, hope's bright visions! Spectral wraiths in white,
For your grim work you flock together; then
Your women's golden hearts bow day and night
Over long agonies of dying men.

Ah, your hands' gestures and your smiling eyes!
Blue, spectral wraiths beside the beds of pain,
You bring your solace to each man who dies
And reassurance to those who remain!

A breeze has risen in the tempest's train
And steals about the fringes of the plain:
Your breath of tenderness, soft as a sigh,
O women, cools our brows as you pass by!

Translated by D.D.R. Owen

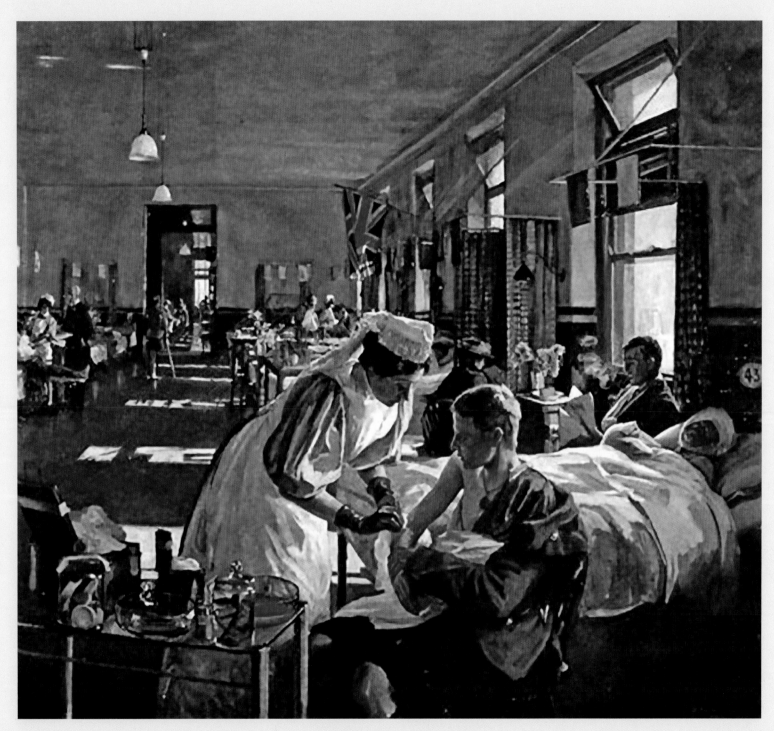

The First Wounded (1919)
John Lavery (1856–1941)

UNDERMANNED

René Arcos

Ripping saws,
Hissing planes,
Flashing chisels,
Volleys of hammers —

A team three hundred strong,
Ablaze with hectic effort,
One short hour after daybreak
Are knee-deep in shavings.

A thousand crosses for Verdun,
A second thousand for Arras,
Another thousand for Soissons,
And a thousand more for Rheims.

A thousand crosses opening their wings
In fright across the charnel-fields —
A thousand crosses opening their wings
In vain, flight taken prisoner.

Get cracking, carpenters!
For by the time tomorrow's dawn
Has limned the eastern sky,
We'll be needing more — more crosses
For stevedores to stack in ships
Bound for Salonika
And the Bosphorus and Africa.

Faster with the hammers,
Faster with the planes —
We've dropped behind,
Demand's outstripped supply.

Put your backs into it, come on,
We need more crosses —
A good ten thousand to replant
A forest now as bare as heathland;
And two million more to wood
That whole disinherited tract of land
From the Alps to the Channel.

Translated by Ian Higgins

Aux Usines de Guerre (1917)
François Flameng (1856–1923)

ALL SOULS' DAY

Lucie Delarue-Mardrus

Public mourning, unconsoled,
A landscape hunching drab and bare
Among the plundering flames of autumn,
Bells tolling, guns' thunder rolling,

All Souls' Day, day of graveside prayer,
Bells tolling, guns' thunder rolling,
Our wearying hearts grown dull and numb
To bells, the alarms, and everywhere

Entire tragedies of lives undone.
In the sad, soft wind, we feel
Brush round us as we kneel
Dead leaves and sundered souls.

At last the bells pause for breath;
But not the drumming, willing guns —
While we are celebrating death,
The distance dins with killing, killing.

Translated by Ian Higgins

Les Victimes du Taube (1915)
Alexis de Broca (1868–1948)

THE PRETTY REDHEAD

Guillaume Apollinaire

Here I am before you all a sensible man

Who knows life and what a living man can know of death

Having experienced love's sorrows and joys

Having sometimes known how to impose my ideas

Adept at several languages

Having travelled quite a bit

Having seen war in the Artillery and the Infantry

Wounded in the head trepanned under chloroform

Having lost my best friends in the frightful conflict

I know of old and new as much as one man can know of the two

And without worrying today about that war

Between us and for us my friends

I am here to judge the long debate between tradition and invention

      Between Order and Adventure

You whose mouth is made in the image of God's

Mouth that is order itself

Be indulgent when you compare us

To those who were the perfection of order

We who look for adventure everywhere

We're not your enemies

We want to give you vast and strange domains

Where mystery in flower spreads out for those who would pluck it

There you may find new fires colours you have never seen before

A thousand imponderable phantasms

Still awaiting reality

We want to explore kindness enormous country where all is still

There is also time which can be banished or recalled

Pity us who fight always at the boundaries

Of infinity and the future

Pity our errors pity our sins

Now it's summer the violent season

And my youth is dead like the springtime

Oh Sun it's time of ardent Reason

     And I am waiting

So I may follow always the noble and gentle shape

That she assumes so I will love her only

She draws near and lures me as a magnet does iron

     She has the charming appearance

     Of a darling redhead

Her hair is golden you'd say

A lovely flash of lightning that lingers on

Or the flame that glows

In fading tea roses

But laugh laugh at me

Men from everywhere especially men from here

For there are so many things I dare not tell you

So many things you would never let me say

Have pity on me

Translated by Anne Hyde Greet

La France Croisée (1914)
Romaine Brooks (1874–1970)

HYMN ONE *from* FIVE HYMNS, AUGUST 1914

Rainer Maria Rilke

For the first time I see you rising,

Hearsaid, remote, incredible War God.

How very thickly terrible action has been sown

Among the peaceful fruits of the fields, action suddenly grown to maturity.

Yesterday it was still small, needed nurture, now it is

Standing there tall as a man: tomorrow

It will outgrow man. For the glowing god

Will suddenly tear his crop

Out of the nation which gave it roots,

   and the harvest will begin.

At last a god. Since we were often no longer able to grasp

The peaceful god, the god of battle suddenly grips us,

Hurling his brand: and over the heart full of homeland

Screams his crimson heaven in which, thunderous,

   he dwells.

Translated by Patrick Bridgwater

An Observer (1915)
E. Handley-Read (1870–1935)

JOURNEY BY NIGHT

Erwin Seligman

Six-coupled horses through the night sail,
Our rattling steel wagon can't tarry,
Across stubble fields, uphill, down dale,
Missiles for murder we carry.

The crescent moon rages, fiery red,
The stars twinkle sad on high.
Blindly preparing a bloody deathbed,
Into the dark night we fly.

Has anyone asked if our mission is right?
Has anyone paused to think?
Onwards we hurry through silent night;
From hissing shells we shrink.

Translated by Francis Clark-Lowes

Mud Road to Passchendaele (1917)
Douglas W. Culham
(1891–1931)

WAR IS COMING

Alfred Lichtenstein

War is coming. There's been peace for too long.

Then things will get serious. Trumpet calls

Will galvanise you. And nights will be ablaze.

You'll freeze in your tent. You'll feel hot all over. You'll go hungry.

Drown. Be blown up. Bleed to death. Fields will rattle to death.

Church-towers will topple. Horizons will be in flames.

Winds will gust. Cities will come crashing down.

The thunder of heavy guns will fill up the horizon.

From the hills all around smoke

Will rise, and shells will explode overhead.

Translated by Patrick Bridgwater

Landscape
Albert Heim
(1849–1937)

LEAVING FOR THE FRONT

Alfred Lichtenstein

Before dying I must just make my poem.
Quiet comrades, don't disturb me.

We are going off to war. Death is our bond.
Oh, if only my girlfriend would stop howling.

What do I matter? I'm happy to go.
Mother's crying. You need to be made of iron.

The sun is falling down on to the horizon.
Soon they'll be throwing me into a nice mass grave.

In the sky the good old sunset is glowing red.
In thirteen days maybe I'll be dead.

Translated by Patrick Bridgwater

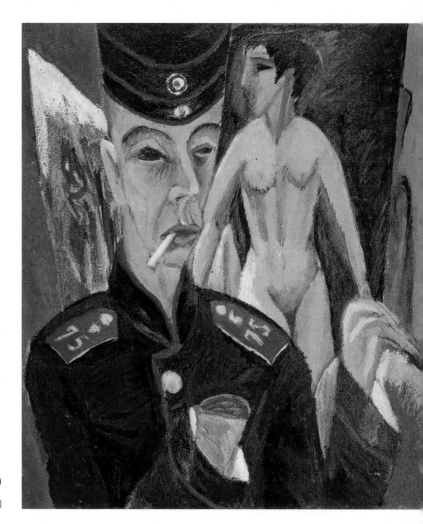

Selbstbildnis als Soldat (Self-portrait as a Soldier) (1915)
Ernst Ludwig Kirchner (1880–1938)

PRAYER BEFORE BATTLE

Alfred Lichtenstein

The men are singing fervently, every man thinking of himself:

God, protect me from accidents,

Father, Son and Holy Ghost,

Don't let shells hit me,

Don't let those bastards, our enemies,

Catch me or shoot me,

Don't let me snuff it like a dog

For my dear Fatherland.

Look, I'd like to go on living,

Milking cows, stuffing girls,

And beating up that blighter Joe,

Getting tight many more times

Before I die like a Christian.

Look, I'll pray well and willingly,

I'll say seven rosaries a day,

If you, God, in your mercy

Will kill my friend Huber, or

Meier, and spare me.

But if I get my lot,

Don't let me be too badly wounded.

Send me a slight leg wound,

A small arm injury,

So that I may return home as a hero

Who has a tale to tell.

Translated by Patrick Bridgwater

Self-Portrait as a Nurse (1915)
Max Beckmann (1884–1950)

THE BATTLE OF SAARBURG

Alfred Lichtenstein

The earth is growing mouldy with mist.
The evening is heavy as lead.
Electrical crackling bursts out all round,
And with a wimper everything breaks asunder.

Like old rags
The villages are smouldering on the horizon.
I am lying God-forsaken
In the rattling front-line.

Many copper enemy birds
Whirl around my heart and head.
I brace myself in the greyness
And face death.

Translated by Patrick Bridgwater

Sunrise (1913)
Otto Dix (1891–1969)

AT THE BEGINNING OF THE WAR

Peter Baum

At the beginning of the war there was a rainbow.

Birds, black, wheeled against grey clouds.

Pigeons shone silver as on their circular journey

They turned through a narrow strip of sunlight.

Battle takes place hard by battle. They lied like troopers.

Row upon row of stoved-in heads fill one with horror.

Shells often explode

As they tumble on beginning to lose velocity.

The shells' pain-bow grows all the time.

Caught between Death and the bow
   of peace,

They clutch their rifle barrels more firmly,
   to defend their homeland,

Spitting at the enemy, leaning on
   one another as they totter,

Tumbling over hills, like waves of the seas,

Staggering on, attracted magnetically
   by Death.

Translated by Patrick Bridgwater

*Den Namenlosen (Those Who Have
Lost Their Names) (1914)*
Albin Egger-Lienz (1868–1926)

FLARES CLIMB HIGH

Peter Baum

Flares climb high up into the sky,

Fireworks extending the night and the sputtering light

Of a decaying moon. With your gun you stand there rigid

As the houses that are lit up.

Flares of bristling tiger's fur.

A trigger is lying in wait for any movement revealed by light

To watchful eye, as though the day

Were not yet dead in which one man was another's prey,

One man's mouth at another's throat,

Until the organ-cry of death is heard.

With eyes wide open you stare at the brilliance

Of the colourful predator, burning brightly

  in the night.

Until night and snow conceal me again,

Grey-green eyes keep these wild melodies awake.

Translated by Patrick Bridgwater

Lichtsignale (The Flare) (1917)
Otto Dix (1891–1969))

GRODEK

Georg Trakl

At nightfall the autumn woods cry out
With deadly weapons and the golden plains,
The deep blue lakes, above which more darkly
Rolls the sun; the night embraces
Dying warriors, the wild lament
Of their broken mouths.
But quietly there in the willow dell
Red clouds in which an angry god resides,
The shed blood gathers, lunar coolness.

All the roads lead to blackest carrion.
Under golden twigs of the night and stars
The sister's shade now sways through the silent copse
To greet the ghosts of the heroes, the bleeding heads;
And softly the dark flutes of autumn sound in the reeds.
O prouder grief! You brazen altars,
Today a great pain feeds the hot flame of the spirit,
The grandsons yet unborn.

Translated by Michael Hamburger

Apocalyptic Landscape (1913)
Ludwig Meidner (1884–1966)

BATTLEFIELD

August Stramm

Lumpish-mellow lulls to sleep the iron

Bleedings filter oozing stains

Rusts crumble

Fleshes slime

Sucking lusts around decay.

Murders' murders

Blinking

Child-like eyes.

Translated by Jeremy Adler

German Shell hits a British Tank,
Battle of the Somme
Fritz Fuhrken (1894–1943)

WAR

August Stramm

Grief graves.

Waiting stares aghast.

Labour shatters.

Giving-birth tenses the limbs.

The hour bleeds.

Question raises its eye.

Time gives birth.

Exhaustion renews death.

Translated by Patrick Bridgwater

The War
Otto Dix (1891–1969)

Baptism of Fire

August Stramm

His body shrinks its loosely-fitting tunic.

His head creeps down into his boots.

Fear

Throttles his gun.

Fears

Rattle,

Rattle shrill,

Rattle swathe,

Rattle stumble,

Rattle,

Trigger off

Shouting

Anger.

His eye

Narrows.

A shot.

Hands grip schnapps.

Defiance loads.

Determination aims

And

A steely look

Quickly

Bags

Another's fate.

Translated by Patrick Bridgwater

First World War German Trench Fighting
Felix Schwormstädt (1870–1938)

I DID NOT LIKE

Hugo Ball

I did not like the Death's Head Hussars
And the mortars with girls' names,
And when at last the great days came,
I quietly slipped away.

I must confess to God and to you, mesdames:
While they were sobbing over biers,
I, like Absalom, was caught by my long hair
In the tree of woe of all their dramas.

You will find in these lines too
Many a martyr play and dashing adventure.
One does not only die from mines and rifles.

One is not only torn to pieces by shells.
My nights were invaded by monsters
Which made me experience Hell.

Translated by Patrick Bridgwater

Dead Soldier
Albin Egger-Lienz (1868–1926)

DANCE OF DEATH, 1916

Hugo Ball

And so we die, and so we die,
We're dying every day
Because it's so easy to die.
In the morning still asleep and dreaming,
Gone by midday.
By evening well and truly buried.

Battle is our brothel.
Our sun is made of blood.
Death is our sign and password.
Wife and child we abandon —
What concern are they of ours?
So long as we can be relied on.

And so we murder, and so we murder.
Every day we murder
Our partners in this dance of death.
Brother, straighten up in front of me,
Brother, your breast!
Brother, you who must fall and die.

We don't grumble, we don't grouse.
We keep our mouths shut all the time
Until our hip-bones are wrenched out.
Our bed is hard,
Our bread is dry.
God is bloody and defiled.

We thank you, we thank you,
Herr Kaiser, for your kindness
In choosing us to die.
Sleep on, sleep peacefully,
Until you are raised from the dead
By our poor bodies pushing up the daisies.

Translated by Patrick Bridgwater

The Wounded Man (1919)
Gert Wollheim (1894–1974)

DYING

Wilhelm Klemm

The blood oozes shyly through the tunic.
The grimy grey limbs quietly wither.
Lips are paler and thinner, noses more pointed.
Perspiration glistens on smoothed brows.

Eyes open, all with the same look.
They all look blue, all peaceful and staring,
Full of infinite remoteness and benignity;
And forgive the world and us these hellish goings-on.

Translated by Patrick Bridgwater

Dead Frenchmen
Albin Egger-Lienz
(1868–1926)

A FIELD HOSPITAL

Wilhelm Klemm

Straw rustles everywhere.
The candle-stumps stare solemnly.
Across the nocturnal vault of the church
Moans and choked words drift aimlessly.

There's a stench of blood, rubbish, shit and sweat.
Bandages ooze beneath torn uniforms.
Clammy, trembling limbs, wasted faces.
Dying heads slump down, half sitting up.

In the distance the storm of the battle thunders on,
Day and night, groaning and grumbling furiously
   and solemnly —
And to the dying men waiting patiently for their graves
It sounds like God's words.

Translated by Patrick Bridgwater

*German Wounded at a
Railway Station*
Felix Schwormstädt
(1870–1938)

DESERTED HOUSE

Wilhelm Klemm

The double doors of the ribs are opening.

Already the blue divans of the lungs are swelling,

And the crimson cushion of the liver, streaked with green,

And between them, resplendent in red lace,

A silent baldachin with four chapels, the heart,

From whose dark tabernacle,

Instead of the hoped-for divine miracle,

Flow only the black roses of the blood.

And in the brain's deathly pale labyrinths,

And in the full vault of the stomach,

And in the master sculpture of solemn bones

You will not find the much-vaunted one.

Already the soul, that eternal nomad,

Has struck its invisible tent.

Translated by Patrick Bridgwater

Thiepval's Ruined Fortress
Albert Heim (1849–1937)

EVENING AT THE FRONT

Wilhelm Klemm

Every evening an officer

Comes into the damp tent and tells us who has fallen.

Every hungry evening when we long lie shivering

There are dead men among us who will die tomorrow.

One had his head blown off,

There a hand is dangling,

Here someone without a foot is wailing,

A captain got it straight in the chest,

And the rain, the rain goes on dripping incessantly.

Throughout the night the cannons go on echoing away.

In the distance villages burn with little red tongues.

O God, how is this destined to end?

Oh questing bullet, when will you come to me?

Translated by Patrick Bridgwater

Evening, After a Push (1919)
Colin Unwin Gill (1892–1940)

AT THE FRONT

Wilhelm Klemm

The countryside is desolate.
　The fields look tear-stained.
A grey cart is going along an evil road.
The roof has slipped off a house.
Dead horses lie rotting in pools.

The brown lines back there are trenches.
On the horizon a farm is taking its time to burn.
Shells explode, echo away pop, pop pauuu.
Cavalrymen disappear slowly in a bare copse.

Clouds of shrapnel burst open and fade away.
A defile takes us in. Infantrymen are halted there, wet and muddy.
Death is as much matter of indifference as the rain which is coming on.
Who cares about yesterday, today, or tomorrow?

And the barbed wire runs across the whole of Europe.
The forts sleep gently.
Villages and towns stink out of their terrible ruins.
Like broken dolls the dead lie between the lines.

Translated by Patrick Bridgwater

Storm and Rainbow, Symbol for Near End of War 1918 (1918)
George Kenner (1888–1971)

THE DEAD SOLDIER

Anton Schnack

Lay there like a solitude, like a pile of stones, whitish, spread out, in much rain.

Why did Death scream at him in the night, that night full of moonlight, warm with the wind?
  Head still full of memories

Of the other side of the Rhine dancing wildly all night long and walking home along Castle Gate;
  in his blood

The fresh wine or the garden with the red lanterns, and the pigeons flying off to their death
  at nightfall …

Children will be solemnly dancing ring-a-ring-o'-roses by the roadside, in April it will rain,
  one evening the air will be full of beetles, but he is just a dark shape; mouth full

Of gentle words, which once hummed a wistful song on the way home one July night. Who killed him?

A man who ran through the sweltering port, who saw nights glittering with stars, through the
  white archway of the balcony, southern with a new moon, red;

Or a man who accompanied circuses to the pandemonium of annual fairs, shabbily dressed,
  in a green jerkin, a bizarre, motley figure? …

That mouth had many things left to say: maybe about gardens strolled through in autumn,
  maybe about ochre-coloured

Cattle, maybe about the poverty of his grey old mother; or that ear, pale, small, still full of thunderstorms
  of deep waves of sound, enjoying hearing again

The black birds in the pear-tree in spring, the shouting of the city children out in the country;

In his eye this: a net full of white fish, bluish-looking stars; was not a Gothic doorway overgrown with ivy,
  gleaming in the dark, once reflected in it? …

Now he is just a dark shape, a death, a thing, a stone, destroyed beyond measure, filling the night
  with its outrage at man's cruelty.

Translated by Patrick Bridgwater

IN THE TRENCHES

Anton Schnack

Everything passes; only death remains, lurking. Everything passed into oblivion: home town,

   the yellow moonlit night, the village dance,

Everything vanished. We are lost men, we are men marked by the red mouth of death,

   we are so dark and so old,

Small as dwarfs. We are astonished that across the expanse of night stars should still sometimes

   sink below the woods,

Blue and deformed, that a flower should still blossom, innocent, among the gleaning bones by the wire.

   We are growing brutish,

We are losing our souls, our sweet, dovelike souls; we are becoming godless and malevolently

   full of blasphemy. In many a deep darkness

Someone began to weep, convulsed, agonised. On many a summer morning when at home blue smoke

   was rising up over the range,

Someone or other lay stiff in the sap trench, with dried blood on his mouth, the shot below his heart.

   One climbed out of the tunnel, badly burned,

Aged, wretched, with one hand missing, many were no longer there because a mine had

   blown them to smithereens in the night …

Prayers? … Oh, often they began to flow from our lips, involuntary, confused, stammering, weary,

When things became too much for us, when everything came to a head: homesickness and the

   bombardment, when gas came billowing over,

Choking us, with yellow poison, when someone suddenly collapsed in a weird silence, quietly,

   soundlessly, wearily,

When smoke, grey, burst from tunnels, smelling of flesh and old cloth … But when a flare

   burst into the night sky,

Green, beautiful, and suspended there, I (who?) would think: of curious wells, red marble amid

   coltsfoot and milkwort,

In distant palazzos in the south; until in the light of flames, gleaming white, I fall into sleep,

   into the straw, overcast by sadness and dejection.

Translated by Patrick Bridgwater

Trenches (1917)
Otto Dix (1891–1969)

STANDING TO

Anton Schnack

I shall go into death as into a doorway filled with summer coolness, the scent of hay, and cobwebs:
  I shall never return

To colourful butterflies, flowers and girls, to dancing and violin music.

Somewhere or other I shall fall on stones, shot in the heart, to join someone else who fell wearily earlier;

I shall have to wander through much smoke and fire and have beautiful eyes like the godly,
  inward-looking,

Dark as velvet, incredibly ardent … What is death? A long sleep. Sleeping eternally deep down
  beneath grass and plants,

Among old gravel? Trumpery. Maybe I shall go to Heaven and enter the snow-white night of God's stars,
  His silken gardens,

His golden evenings, His lakes … I shall lie beneath the open sky, looking strange, ancient, portentous,

My mind once again filled with days out in the Tyrol, fishing in the Isar, snowfields,
  the noise and excitement of the annual fair

In prosperous villages in Franconia, prayers, songs, cuckoos calling, woods, and a train journey
  along the Rhine at night.

Then I shall become like evening, secret, dark, puzzling, mysterious, benighted;
  then I shall be like earth, lifeless and void,

And totally removed from the things around me: days, animals, tears, deep blue dreams,
  hunting, merrymaking.

I shall go into death as into the doorway of my house, with a shot in the heart, painless, strangely small.

Translated by Patrick Bridgwater

A German Attack on a Wet Morning, April 1918
Harold Sandys Williamson (1892–1978)

POETS' BIOGRAPHIES

BRITISH POETS

Herbert Asquith (1881–1947), the son of Herbert Henry Asquith, Prime Minister until December 1916, was educated at Winchester and Balliol College, Oxford. He was one of four brothers who served in the British Army in the First World War. He served as a captain in the Royal Artillery, and was wounded in the leg so severely that it had to be amputated. His brother, Raymond, was killed in the war.

Laurence Binyon (1869–1943) was born in Lancaster and educated at Trinity College, Oxford. He was a poet, art historian and translator. He worked for forty years at the British Museum, first in the Department of Printed Books and then as Keeper of the Department of Oriental Prints and Books. He wrote the poem 'For the Fallen', now quoted in Remembrance Day services, in the first weeks of the war. For a short time during the war he was a stretcher-bearer in France.

Edmund Blunden (1896–1974), born in Yalding, Kent, was a poet, academic and critic. He was educated at Christ's Hospital School, and went directly into the army in 1915. He experienced some of the worst fighting on the Western Front, where he suffered in a gas attack. He was awarded the Military Cross. Most of his war poems were written in the 1920s, and he wrote a prose account of his experiences in the First World War, *Undertones of War*, in 1928. He was Professor of Poetry at Oxford University from 1966 to 1968.

Robert Bridges (1844–1930), born in Walmer, Kent, and educated at Eton and Corpus Christi College, Oxford, was a medical doctor until 1881. His first volume of poetry was published in 1873. Bridges became a popular and respected poet, and was appointed Poet Laureate in 1913. He was a passionate supporter of the First World War, seeing it as 'a holy war … a fight of good against evil'.

Vera Brittain (1893–1970) was born in Newcastle-under-Lyme. She spent just one year at Somerville College, Oxford, before working as a nurse in England, France and Malta. Her war experiences, and the loss of a close friend, her fiancé and her brother in the war, proved traumatic. These experiences are reflected in both her poetry and her famous biography, *Testament of Youth*, which she wrote to record what she saw as the effect of the war on her generation. She was a pacifist, a feminist, and an advocate of the League of Nations.

Rupert Brooke (1887–1915) was born at Rugby and educated at Rugby School and King's College, Cambridge. He was a friend of Edward Marsh, the private secretary of Winston Churchill. Brooke joined the navy and witnessed the siege of Antwerp before writing his famous set of five sonnets entitled '1914'. In 1915 he set sail to take part in the Gallipoli Campaign, but before it started he died on board ship of acute blood poisoning following a mosquito bite. He was buried on the Greek island of Skyros.

Leslie Coulson (1889–1916), born in Kilburn, London, worked as a journalist before the war. He saw service as an ordinary foot soldier in Malta, Egypt, Gallipoli and the Western Front. He took part in the first day of the Battle of the Somme. He was killed in the battle of Le Transloy in October 1916.

Robert Graves (1895–1985) was born in London and educated at Charterhouse. His mother was German. At the outbreak of the First World War, Graves enlisted almost immediately, taking a commission in the Royal Welch Fusiliers. At the Battle of the Somme he suffered major physical injuries and shellshock. During a long period of convalescence from 1916 to 1917 he published three volumes of war poetry, *Over the Brazier, Goliath and David* and *Fairies and Fusiliers*. He wrote a bestselling autobiographical account of the war, *Goodbye to All That*, in 1929. He was Oxford Professor of Poetry from 1961 to 1966.

Ivor Gurney (1890–1937), a prolific poet and composer, was born in Gloucester and educated at King's School, Gloucester and the Royal College of Music. He volunteered to fight in 1914 and fought on the Western Front, where he suffered sufficiently in a gas attack to be sent to a hospital near Edinburgh. His mental illness, which had started before the war, developed rapidly, and from 1922 he was confined to a mental hospital.

Thomas Hardy (1840–1928) was born at near Dorchester and educated at a private school. He was a prolific poet, but is best known for his enduring novels. When the First World War broke out he responded enthusiastically to the government's call to notable writers to write in support of the war. However, by the end of the war his war poetry had a regretful and bewildered tone.

Rudyard Kipling (1865–1936) was born in Bombay and educated in Southsea and the United Services College, Westwood Ho! He was a hugely successful author, especially of children's books. At the start of the war the British Government enlisted him to work as a propagandist, and he was appointed Director of Propaganda to the British Colonies. He was devastated by the death of his only son in the Battle of Loos in 1915.

Joseph Lee (1876–1949), born in Dundee, was a newspaper cartoonist and journalist. He was almost forty when he volunteered to fight in the First World War. He was eventually captured by the Germans, an experience he was later to describe in his book, *A Captive in Carlsruhe*. He published two volumes of war poetry.

Eileen Newton (1883–1930) worked for a solicitor in Whitby, and wrote poems and songs in her spare time, including the lyrics for the famous Victorian parlour song 'Somewhere a Voice is Calling'. Her fiancé enlisted in the navy and was lost at sea. Her work was widely praised and published in leading periodicals.

Robert Nichols (1893–1944), a poet and dramatist, was educated at Winchester and Trinity College, Oxford. He fought in France for only three weeks before being sent home permanently suffering from shellshock. His two anthologies of poetry of the First World War were very popular. He was friends with fellow war poets Siegfried Sassoon and Rupert Brooke.

Alfred Noyes (1880–1958) was born in Wolverhampton and attended Exeter College, Oxford, but left prematurely. He was a successful playwright, novelist and academic as well as being a prolific poet. His most famous poem is 'The Highwayman'. He became a Roman Catholic in 1926.

Wilfred Owen (1893–1918) was born in Oswestry, Shropshire, and educated at Birkenhead Institute and Shrewsbury Technical College. Now widely regarded as the greatest English war poet of the First World War, his reputation grew slowly from obscurity at the time of his death, at the age of 25, to his present-day status. From the age of nineteen Owen wrote a good deal of experimental poetry. From 1911 to 1913 he was a lay assistant to the vicar of Dunsden near Reading, and from 1913 to 1915 he worked as a private language tutor in the south of France. He came home to England and volunteered to fight on 21 October 1915. He was horrified by his front-line experience and after suffering shellshock (PTSD) was sent to Craiglockhart War Hospital in Edinburgh. It was here that he met Siegfried Sassoon who encouraged him and helped him to develop his war poetry. Owen returned to the front in September 1918 and was awarded the Military Cross in October. He was killed near the village of Ors on 4 November 1918.

Isaac Rosenberg (1890–1918) was born to Jewish pacifist parents in Bristol and grew up in the East End of London. His prime interest was painting and he attended the Slade School of Art. Poverty and desire to support his mother led him to volunteer in October 1915. He served in France from June 1916 until 1 April 1918, with only ten days leave in this period. Many of his war poems were written at the Front, a factor which may have helped to give them their graphic immediacy.

Siegfried Sassoon (1886–1967) was educated at Marlborough and Clare College, Cambridge. For a time he led the life of a gentleman of leisure, loving cricket and foxhunting. Anticipating the start of the war, he volunteered on 3 August 1914. Initially he revelled in army life and wrote enthusiastic poetry about the war. However, early in 1916 he became critical of the war and from this time some of his poetry was satirical. He had a reputation for wild courage and was awarded the Military Cross. He was shot in the shoulder, resulting in his return to England in 1917. In the summer of 1917 he made a public protest about the conduct of the war, which resulted in the authorities sending him to Craiglockhart War Hospital in Edinburgh.

He saw further military service in Ireland, Palestine and France before receiving a graze wound to his head in July 1918. After the war he wrote more poetry, volumes of autobiographical accounts of his experiences and was, for a brief time, literary editor of the *Daily Herald*.

Edward Shilito (1872–1948) was born in Wakefield and educated at Mansfield College, Oxford. He was a free Church minister in the south of England.

Charles Sorley (1895–1915) was born in Aberdeen and educated at Marlborough, University College, Oxford, and at Schwerin and Jena in Germany. He loved Germany and the Germans and hated the idea of fighting against them. He consciously yielded to the psychological pressure to enlist and was quickly promoted to the rank of captain. He was killed on 13 October 1915 at the age of twenty.

Arthur Graeme West (1891–1917), educated at Blundell's and Oxford, joined the army in February 1915. By mid-1916 he had lost his religious faith and, possibly influenced by the pacifist philosopher, Bertrand Russell, felt that he should publicly protest about the war or desert, and berated himself for lacking the courage to do either. He was killed on 3 April 1917 at Bapaume.

IRISH POETS

Lord Dunsany (1878–1957), the pen name of Edward Plunkett, 18th Baron of Dunsany, was a prolific author of more than eighty books including plays, novels, essays and hundreds of short stories. He was educated at Cheam, Eton and Sandhurst. He was acquainted with many literary figures in Ireland and was a supporter of Francis Ledwidge. He fought in the Boer War and on the front line in the First World War.

John Hewitt (1907–1987) was born in Belfast and educated at Queen's University, Belfast. He worked in the Belfast Museum and Art Gallery. In 1957 he moved to Coventry, where he became Director of the Herbert Art Gallery and Museum.

Thomas Kettle (1880–1916) was born in Dublin and educated at University College Dublin. He was a prominent politician and eloquent advocate of home rule for all Ireland, a barrister, economist and prolific writer. He fought with the Irish Brigade in the First World War and was killed in action.

Francis Ledwidge (1887–1917) was born in Slane, County Meath, one of nine children in a very poor family. He left school at thirteen and worked at various labouring jobs. Once he was sacked for organising a strike. He was an active Irish nationalist. Initially he was against fighting on the British side in the First World War, but he volunteered on 24 October 1914 to fight in Lord Dunsany's regiment in the 5th Battalion Royal Inniskilling Fusiliers. He fought in the Battle of Gallipoli, and was killed in the Battle of Passchendaele.

Padraic Pearse (1879–1916) was born in Dublin. He was a barrister, journalist, essayist and a leading advocate of home rule for Ireland. He was one of the leaders of the Easter Rising in 1916 and was executed by the British.

George 'AE' Russell (1867–1935) was born in Lurgan, County Armagh and educated in Dublin at Rathmines School and the Metropolitan School of Art. He was an Irish nationalist, economist, mystic, writer and painter, and a lifelong friend of W.B. Yeats. His home in Dublin was for a long time a meeting place for intellectuals, artists and political thinkers.

Katharine Tynan (1861–1931) was born in Clondalkin, County Dublin and educated at Siena Convent, Drogheda. She was a prolific novelist. A staunch supporter of British action in the war, she had two sons serving in the front line.

W.B. Yeats (1865–1939) was born in Sandymount, County Dublin, but grew up in County Sligo. He was educated in Dublin at the Erasmus Smith High School and the Metropolitan School of Art. Yeats was the most gifted Irish poet of his generation and a noted playwright. He was a leading figure in the Irish Literary Revival. He had great sympathy with the Irish Nationalist cause but was less enamoured of nationalist activism. He was interested in legends, mysticism, spiritualism, astrology and the occult. In 1916 he married 25-year-old Georgie Hyde-Lees, with whom he had two children. He was elected twice to the Senate of the new Irish Free State, in 1922 and 1925. He was awarded the Nobel Prize for Literature in 1923.

AUSTRALIAN POETS

James Drummond Burns (1895–1915) was a corporal in the First Battalion Australian Infantry. He was killed at Gallipoli on 18 September 1915.

Leon Gellert (1892–1977) was born at Walkerville, South Australia. He fought at Gallipoli, and his collection of war poetry, *Songs of a Campaign*, received critical approval. He wrote further poems, and worked as a teacher, journalist and critic.

Mary Gilmore (1865–1962) was born at Cotta Walla, near Goulburn, New South Wales. She taught in numerous schools and was moved by the plight of the working class. In 1896 she emigrated to Paraguay but returned to Australia in 1902, where she lived with her husband on an isolated farm in the Casterton district of western Victoria. She was a powerful campaigner for the welfare of the young and old, sick and helpless and underprivileged. In her popular press articles she railed against privilege and corruption in high places. She also wrote some 1,500 pages of verse. Such was her standing in popular esteem that she was given a state funeral.

Frederic Manning (1882–1935) was born in Sydney. He had limited formal education because he suffered from bronchial asthma. At the age of fifteen he moved to England, where he educated himself. He enlisted with the British Army at the start of the First World War and served on the Somme and on the Ancre Front. He was then moved to Ireland to help deal with the unrest. He is best known for his highly regarded autobiographical war novel, *The Middle Parts of Fortune*.

Furnley Maurice (real name Frank Wilmot) (1881–1942) was born in Collingwood, Melbourne. He began his career as an errand boy in Cole's Book Arcade in Melbourne. By stages he rose to become manager of Melbourne University Press. He published several volumes of poetry and became an authority on Australian literature. His war poetry is critical of the glamourising of war.

Vance Palmer (1885–1959) was born at Bundaberg, Queensland. In 1905 he became a journalist in London, returning to Australia in 1912. In 1914 he was in London where he married. He returned again to Australia in September 1915. He opposed conscription, but nevertheless volunteered for the Australian Imperial Force in 1918. He was sent overseas but was too late to see action. Returning to Australia he worked as a journalist, critic, essayist, novelist, biographer and promoter of Australian literature. He became one of Australia's leading literary figures.

Banjo Paterson (1864–1941) was born Andrew Barton Paterson at Narambla Station near Orange, New South Wales. He grew up in the bush, and went to school in the small town of Binalong before moving to Sydney where he attended Sydney Grammar School. He qualified as a solicitor in Sydney. His early experiences furnished him with a wealth of knowledge and understanding of Australian people and Australian life which he put to good use in *The Man from Snowy River and Other Verses*, which brought him instant fame. He was a war correspondent in the Boer War, and editor of the *Sydney Evening News*. In the First World War he was first a war correspondent, but dissatisfied with this he joined active service. Initially he was an ambulance driver with the Australian Voluntary Hospital at Wimereux. He returned to Australia in 1915 as an honorary vet, and travelled with three cargoes of horses to Africa, China and Egypt. He joined the second Remount Unit, Australian Imperial Force in late 1915 and became commanding officer of the unit in Cairo. At this time he wrote more poetry, short stories and novels. He is the author of 'Waltzing Matilda', Australia's national song, and an iconic figure in Australian culture.

Frank Westbrook (1889–1976), born at South Yarra, in Victoria, was a trumpeter in the Second Field Artillery Brigade. His unit sailed from Australia on 20 October 1914 heading for Egypt, prior to fighting at Gallipoli for the duration of that campaign. It was here that his poems were written.

Canadian Poets

Alfred Bryan (1871–1958), born in Brantford, Ontario, was a highly successful lyricist. He moved to New York and produced lyrics for many Broadway shows before moving to Hollywood to write lyrics for Hollywood musicals. His song, 'I Didn't Raise My Boy to be a Soldier', sold 650,000 copies in the United States in three months.

Helena Coleman (1860–1953) was born in Newcastle, Ontario. She was a successful journalist and published a single volume of war poetry in 1917, *Marching Men: War Verses*.

Elspeth Honeyman's (1895–*c*.1950) poem, 'Canada's Answer', appeared in *Canadian Poems of the Great War*, edited by John W. Garvin and published in 1918. From this we learn that she was born in Ladnor, British Columbia and educated at Yale and the University of British Columbia. Her poems were published in Britain and the United States as well as Canada.

John Daniel Logan (1869–1929), born in Antigonish, Nova Scotia, was educated at Dalhousie University and Harvard University. He was an early authority of Canadian literature, as well as being a successful businessman and music critic. He volunteered to fight in the First World War at the age of forty-nine.

Isabel Ecclestone Mackay (1875–1928) was born in Woodstock, Ontario and educated at the Woodstock Collegiate Institute. She was a novelist and playwright and a prolific poet. She was the first president of the Canadian Women's Press Club.

John McCrae (1872–1918), born in Guelph, Ontario, studied medicine at the University of Toronto. He fought in the Boer War and was a field surgeon in the First World War in France. His poem, 'In Flanders Fields', was written near Ypres in the spring of 1915 and first published in *Punch* magazine in London in December of that year, gaining immediate popularity. Shortly before his death from pneumonia, McCrae was appointed Medical Consultant to all the British armies in France.

Marjorie Pickthall (1883–1922) was born in Gunnersby, Middlesex, England, and moved to Canada with her parents when she was six years old. She showed early promise as a poet and novelist. She lived in England during the First World War, trained as an ambulance driver, and worked as a farm labourer and finally as a librarian in South Kensington Meteorological Office. She returned to Canada in 1920 where she lived for the remainder of her short life.

Frank Prewett (1893–1962), born at Kenilworth near Mount Forest, Ontario, attended University College, University of Toronto. He enlisted in 1915 and fought in France in the Canadian Expeditionary Force. He was severely wounded and shell-shocked in 1918. At Craiglockhart War Hospital in Edinburgh he met Siegfried Sassoon who encouraged him with his poetry.

Frederick George Scott (1861–1944), born in Montreal, was educated at Bishop's College, Lennoxville, Quebec and later studied theology at King's College, London. He eventually became Archdeacon of Quebec City Cathedral. During the First World War he was chaplain to the Canadian First Division where he became famous for his exceptional courage. Two of his sons were killed in the war. He was a popular and highly regarded poet.

Robert Service (1874–1958) was born in Preston, Lancashire, England. In 1896 he moved to Canada and worked on a farm near Duncan, Vancouver Island. He travelled in south-western USA and Mexico before returning to ranch work on Vancouver Island. He enjoyed immense success as the author of humorous and melodramatic ballads. In 1912 he became a journalist in Eastern Europe and spent the first two years of the First World War as a war correspondent and stretcher bearer in France.

Bernard Freeman Trotter (1890–1917) was born in Toronto and educated at McMaster University in Toronto. He attempted to enlist in the Canadian Army at the outbreak of war but was rejected on grounds of poor health. He travelled to England and succeeded in joining the British Army. He arrived in France in December 1916 with the Leicestershire Regiment. He was killed by a shell on 7 May 1917.

FRENCH POETS

Edmond Adam (1889–1918) was born in Libourne and studied civil engineering in Paris. He became a roads engineer in Bordeaux in 1910. Just as he was finishing his National Service war broke out and he volunteered for the front line where he remained from December 1914 to 24 August 1918 when he was killed at La Veuve. He was a talented, well-read and highly experimental writer of poetry and a fierce critic of the war.

Guillaume Apollinaire (1880–1918) was born in Rome as Wilhelm Apollinaris Kostrowitzky. His mother was Polish and his father may have been Italian. He was educated at schools in Monaco, Nice and Cannes, but did not qualify for a university education. From the age of nineteen he travelled around Europe and lived for a time in Berlin, Prague and London before settling in the city he loved most, Paris. He was an innovative and enthusiastic literary and artistic thinker, and a major French language poet. As a journalist and critic he was an influential promoter of Futurist and Cubist artists. Initially he was enthusiastic about the war and loved the noise and spectacle. He was invalided out of the war in 1916 after suffering a serious head wound, and died from influenza two days before the end of the war.

René Arcos (1881–1959) was born in Paris. He had faith in mankind's possible progress towards happiness while at the same time being hostile to the alienation he saw forced on individuals by modern society. Early in the war he was seriously injured and invalided out of the army. He wrote passionately against the war and had a concern for the suffering of individuals and their personal responsibilities for their actions.

Nicolas Beaudin (1881–1960) had an almost religious devotion to France, seeing his country as chosen by God to save culture and civilisation. He was more than willing to sacrifice himself for France and fought as a soldier during the war. Before the war he had been an experimental, avant-garde writer, but his war poems are written in traditional verse forms, sometimes suggesting religious texts and styles.

Jean-Marc Bernard (1881–1915) was born in Valence-sur-Rhône. He was exempted from National Service on health grounds. He worked in banks and bookshops before founding *Les Guêpes*, a satirical and critical magazine aimed at promoting traditional, classical forms of writing. He volunteered to fight at the beginning of the war and was sent to the front in April 1915. On 9 July 1915 he was killed by a shell.

Jean-Pierre Calloc'h (1888–1917), the son of a fisherman, was born on the island of Groix, southwest of Brittany. He was educated first at Catholic schools on the island and later at Vannes. After National Service he studied for a degree in Paris. He was passionate about the Breton language and culture, and at one time thought of becoming a missionary. At the start of the war he immediately volunteered to fight, believing that he was defending 'civilisation and Christianity'. He was killed by a shell on 10 April 1917.

Marc de Larreguy de Civrieux (1885–1916) volunteered to fight and was posted to the front in July 1915. Within a few months he was writing poetry opposing the war and the propaganda which accompanied it. He claimed that he was writing what all soldiers at the front were thinking. He was killed near Verdun on 18 November 1916.

Henriette Charasson (1884–1972) wrote a series of poems about the war, expressing a range of feelings about it, many of them showing a consciousness of the passive helplessness of women in war. What dominated her thinking, however, was the disappearance of her brother, Camille, at the front.

Lucie Delarue-Mardrus (1874–1945) was born and lived in Normandy. She was a poet, novelist and journalist. During the war she worked for a time as a Red Cross nurse. At the start of the war she was an enthusiastic supporter of it. Never losing her commitment to the cause, she became increasingly saddened by the loss of so many men.

Albert-Paul Granier (1888–1917), born in Le Croisic, trained as a solicitor in Nantes, and was a keen sportsman and enthusiastically interested in the arts. He was fascinated by language and poetry and wrote with originality and sophistication. He fought with distinction in the war and was awarded the Légion d'Honneur. In August 1917, when Granier was acting as an artillery observer, his plane was shot down. His body was never found.

Anna de Noailles (1876–1933), a comtesse, was a thoughtful and sensitive supporter of the war and very conscious of the human costs. Her only son was born in 1900 and her husband served at the front from the outbreak of the war.

Cécile Périn (1877–1959) was born in Reims. Her volume of poetry, *Les Captives*, was published in 1919. It explores a wide range of women's experiences and feelings in relation to the war.

Gaston de Ruyter (1895–1918) was born at Huy, near Liège in Belgium. He volunteered for the infantry at the outbreak of war and wrote his poetry either in the trenches or on leave close behind the front. In March 1918 he started training as a fighter pilot. He was shot down in October 1918.

Henriette Sauret (1890–1976) delighted in life and human creativity. She was bitterly opposed to the glorification of war and those who died in battle. She regretted the helplessness of women in times of war and used her poetry as a form of protest. Some of her poetry appeared in censored form and many of her lines have not been recovered.

FRENCH POETRY TRANSLATOR

Ian Higgins (*b.*1941) was educated at Wyggeston Grammar School, Leicester, and Exeter College, Oxford. He taught French at St Andrews University from 1966 to 1998. He has published books and articles on Francis Ponge, French Resistance poetry, Great War French poetry, and translation methodology. Among his translations of twentieth-century French poetry, short stories and art criticism are Pierre Seghers's *Piranèse* and André Verdet's *Chagall Méditerranéen*. He is currently translating Albert-Paul Granier's *Les Coqs et les Vautours* (1917) for Saxon Books.

GERMAN POETS

Hugo Ball (1886–1927) studied philosophy at Munich, Heidelberg and Basel Universities. For a time he was a theatrical producer. He was intensely patriotic but horrified by the war. He felt compelled to write critically of the war and in 1915 moved to Switzerland in order to be able to write freely against the violence which so disturbed him. He was a founder of the Dada movement, and a friend of the novelist Hermann Hesse.

Peter Baum (1869–1916) was born in Elberfeld into a strictly Protestant family. After dabbling unsuccessfully in publishing he became a poet and a novelist. At the age of forty-five he became a stretcher bearer on the Western Front and was killed by shrapnel in June 1916 whilst digging a grave.

Wilhelm Klemm (1881–1968) was a qualified doctor, and at the age of thirty-three, in August 1914, was called up to work as a field surgeon in General von Hausen's Third Army in Flanders. His earliest war poems were published in *Die Aktion*, the anti-war literary magazine. He ceased writing war poetry after the spring of 1915.

Alfred Lichtenstein (1889–1914) was a Prussian Jew, born in Berlin. He studied law, but was more interested in writing and the theatre. He began his one-year conscription to the army in October 1913.

In August 1914 his regiment was sent to the front where he died from wounds at Vermandovillers on the Somme on 24 September 1914 at the age of twenty-five.

Rainer Maria Rilke (1875–1926) was born in Prague. He attended a military school, but was not suited to the army. He attended the School of Commerce at Linz and found himself unsuited to commerce. In 1895 he began to study philosophy at Prague University but gave this up after a year and moved to Munich to become a writer. Rilke is rated as one of the great poets of the twentieth century, noted for his superb ability to handle language, his complexity and the difficulty, or even obscurity, of his poetry.

Anton Schnack (1892–1973), born in Rieneck, was a journalist, theatre critic, short story writer, novelist and poet. He served in both world wars, and was wounded in 1916. Though virtually unknown in Germany, he is ranked by Patrick Bridgwater as 'one of the two unambiguously great poets of the war on the German side'. He wrote many war poems, mostly in sonnet form, and describing a wide range of war experience at the front. In 1933, along with eighty or so other writers, he pledged his support for Adolf Hitler.

Erwin Seligman (1893–1989) was born into a Jewish family in Hamburg. Though educated as a Jew, he later became an atheist. He studied law at Freiburg University. He served in a field artillery unit on both the Western and Eastern Fronts, and was almost killed near Verdun when a piece of shrapnel entered his head. He left Germany in 1939, settled in Britain, and for a while served in the British Army.

August Stramm (1874–1915) was born in Munster and worked as a postal official, achieving a senior administrative rank. He wrote plays in the Expressionist manner. His use of language was experimental and revolutionary. He was a frequent contributor to the modernist magazine, *Der Sturm*. At the outbreak of the war, Stramm was a captain in the reserve, becoming commander of a regiment when he was called up. He served first on the Western Front where he felt engulfed by the horror of war. Nevertheless, he was a passionately effective and decorated officer. He was killed on the Russian Front on 27 May 1915.

Georg Trakl (1887–1914) was born in Salzburg and trained as a pharmacist. In his late teens he became increasingly introspective, taking to heavy drinking and drugs. He wrote plays and book reviews and some hundred poems. In August 1914 he was a pharmacist attached to the Medical Corps of the Austrian Army. He found his duties, especially when there were insufficient drugs to treat patients, overwhelming. As a result he was sent to Cracow and detained by medical authorities for observation. He died from an overdose of cocaine in November 1914 at the age of twenty-seven.

GERMAN POETRY TRANSLATOR

Patrick Bridgwater (*b.*1931), Emeritus Professor of German at the University of Durham, is known in the present context for his pioneering work on the German and Austrian poetry of the First World War, which includes a critical study, *The German Poets of the First World War* (1985), an early anthology, *German Poems of the First World War* (1965), and a series of essays on German and Austrian war painting. He also writes on the problems inherent in painting modern war, given as papers in international conferences.

Artists' Biographies

Cecil Charles Windsor Aldin (1870–1935), a British artist and illustrator, is best known for his paintings and sketches of animals, sports, and rural life. He studied anatomy at South Kensington and animal painting under William Frank Calderon. Early influences included Randolph Caldecott and John Leech.

Cyril Barraud (1877–1965) was born in Barnes, London, and moved to Canada in 1913 with his art skills fully developed. He soon began exhibiting with the Royal Canadian Academy and taught at the Winnipeg School of Art where he influenced a number of subsequently locally-important artists. His metiers were landscape painting and etching. He left for England with the Canadian Expeditionary Force in 1915 as a lieutenant in the 43rd Battalion. By 1916 he was in France, where he did much painting of the war-torn landscape and suffering, particularly at Ypres, Mont St Eloy and Vlamerlinghe. He remained in Britain after demobilisation.

Alfred Théodore Joseph Bastien (1873–1955) was a Belgian artist, academic and soldier. He attended the Académie Royale des Beaux-Arts in Ghent and the Académie Royale des Beaux-Arts in Brussels, before moving to Paris to study at the École des Beaux-Arts, where he was living when hostilities broke out in 1914.

Max Beckmann (1884–1950), German expressionist painter and graphic artist, studied painting at the Weimar School of Art, and from 1904 to 1914 in Berlin he participated in the Secession movement. The transition

from classicicism to realism came in the First World War years, when Beckmann's shocking experiences as a corpsman in Belgium and France led him to embrace a cold reality and a dreamworld quality, marking him as one of the foremost masters of the modern era.

Walter Armiger Bowring (1874–1931) was born in Auckland, New Zealandt. He worked as a cartoonist before moving to London in 1905 to study with William Orpen and Augustus John. On his return to New Zealand he painted portraits of many public figures.

Muriel Brandt (1909–1981) studied at the Belfast College of Art and at the Royal College of Art in London, where she was elected Associate Royal College of Art in 1937. As well as working in oil and watercolours, she painted mural decorations, portraits and landscapes, and was commissioned to paint the portraits of many Irish notables.

Alexis de Broca (1868–1948), French landscape and portrait painter, studied in Paris and spent extended periods in Morocco, painting traditional scenes and figures in a light plein air style.

Romaine Brooks (1874–1970), born Beatrice Romaine Goddard, was an American painter who worked mostly in Paris and Capri. In 1914 she painted 'The Cross of France', a much-reproduced symbolic image of France at war, showing a Red Cross nurse looking off to the side with a resolute expression while Ypres burns in the distance behind her.

Edgar Bundy (1862–1922) was an historical and genre painter and watercolourist, born in Brighton. He spent much time as a boy in the studio of Alfred Stevens, but was otherwise self-taught. He exhibited at the Royal Academy from 1881 and at the Paris Salon from 1907.

Charles Ernest Butler (1864–1933) was a London-based painter of portraits, mythological subjects and landscapes. Born at St Leonards-on-Sea, Sussex, he studied at St John's Wood School of Art and at the Royal Academy, exhibiting there from 1889 to 1918.

George Edmund Butler (1872–1936), British-born New Zealand landscape and portrait painter specialising in oils and watercolours, studied at the Lambeth School of Art, the Académie Julian in Paris, and the Antwerp Academy before returning to New Zealand in 1900. In 1918 the New Zealand Expeditionary Force War Museum Committee approached Butler to be an official New Zealand war artist; he was appointed with the honorary rank of captain in September 1918 and joined the New Zealand Division in France later that same month. He carried a sketchbook in which he made drawings of actual operations and war scenes, often under fire, which were later used as the basis for his paintings. After the Armistice he returned to sketch all the New Zealand battlefield sites in Belgium and France.

Mildred Anne Butler (1858–1941) was born in Thomastown, Co. Kilkenny, Ireland, and travelled to Brussels and Paris in the early 1880s, studying alongside Walter Osborne and John Lavery. Her works were exhibited in the USA and Japan, and the Kilkenny Museum of Art was renamed The Butler Gallery in her honour.

George Clausen (1852–1944), born in London, was the son of a decorative artist, attended the design classes at the South Kensington Schools, and worked in the studio of Edwin Long, Bouguereau and Robert-Fleury. He became one of the foremost modern painters of landscape and of peasant life, influenced to a certain extent by the impressionists. He was an official war artist during World War I; during the war his daughter's fiancé was killed, which inspired his painting 'Youth Mourning'.

Douglas W. Culham (1891–1931), Canadian artist, served in the 3rd Canadian Division Ammunition Column, which brought ammunition nightly to the 18-pounder batteries during the Battle of Passchendaele in October and November 1917.

Frank Rossiter Crozier (1883–1948), Australian artist, studied at the National Gallery of Victoria Art School and was a member of the Charterisville artists' colony in Heidelberg. He enlisted with the Australian Imperial Force in March 1915, and he served in the 22nd Battalion in Egypt and on the Gallipoli peninsula. Whilst at Gallipoli he was approached by journalist C.E.W. Bean to help illustrate *The Anzac Book*, a collection of short stories and illustrations for the troops. Crozier served in France in 1917, notably in the area around Pozières, but it was only in 1918 that he was made an official war artist. While other war artists were civilians who were attached to the army and given honorary rank, Crozier was already a serving soldier. After the war he made a living as a prolific painter of farm scenes and landscapes.

Maurice Galbraith Cullen (1866–1934) was a Canadian artist who grew up in St John's, Newfoundland, and is best-known for his winter landscapes. From January 1918, he served with Canadian forces in the First World War, where he came to the attention of Lord Beaverbrook, who arranged for him to be commissioned as an official war artist.

Lilian Lucy Davidson (1893–1954) was born in Bray, Co. Wicklow. She studied at the National College of Art and Design, and began exhibiting with the Water Colour Society of Ireland when she was nineteen. In 1914 she met Mainie Jellet, with whom she held a joint exhibition in 1920 at her studio in Earlsfort Terrace, Dublin. Among her portrait subjects were Jack B. Yeats, Sarah Purser, George 'AE' Russell, Austin Clarke and Joseph Holloway

Wilhelm Heinrich Otto Dix (1891–1969), German painter and printmaker, is particularly noted for his ruthless and harshly realistic depictions of Weimar society and the brutality of war. In 1914 he volunteered enthusiastically for the German Army, and was assigned to a field artillery regiment in Dresden. In autumn 1915 he was assigned as a non-commissioned officer of a machine-gun unit in the Western front and took part in the Battle of the Somme, and he also saw action on the Eastern Front. He was profoundly affected by the sights of the war, and represented his traumatic experiences in many subsequent works, including a portfolio of fifty etchings entitled *Der Krieg*. When the Nazis came to power, they regarded Dix as a degenerate artist and had him sacked from his post as an art teacher at the Dresden Academy. In 1939 he was arrested on a trumped-up charge of being involved in a plot against Hitler, but was later released. During the Second World War Dix was conscripted into the *Volkssturm*. He was captured by French troops at the end of the war and released in February 1946. He continued to produce powerful images of the sufferings of war until his death.

Charles Edward Dixon (1872–1934) was a British maritime painter whose work was highly successful and regularly exhibited at the Royal Academy. Several of his paintings are held by the National Maritime Museum, and he was a regular contributing artist to magazines and periodicals.

Albin Egger-Lienz (1868–1926) worked mostly in Vienna, and was a member of the Vienna Secession movement. At the outbreak of the Great War he signed up for the Egger-Lienz Standschützen, where he was occupied mostly in trench digging and painting camouflage. When it was realised that he had a weak heart, he was moved out of active service and became artistic adviser to the War Office in Bolzano. In 1916 he spent time at the front working as a war artist, later using his sketches as the basis for a series of powerful studio paintings.

Adolf Erbslöh (1881–1947) was born in New York, but his family returned to Germany in 1901. He was drafted to the military in 1914, where he served as a war painter at the western front until the end of the war. After the war he travelled widely, producing numerous pictures of mountainous landscapes. Many of his paintings remain unfinished, and he signed hardly any of them.

Conrad Felixmüller (1897–1977), born Conrad Felix Müller and later changing his name, attended the School of Applied Arts in Dresden. He met Arnold Schönberg in 1914 and immediately became a member of the Dresden Secession. He is one of the more important artists of the Weimar Era. During the First World War, he served in the military as a medical aide, and like his colleagues George Grosz and John Heartfield was galvanised by the social changes that swept Germany in the early 1920s. In 1933 forty of his paintings were included in the Nazi exhibition 'Reflections of Decay' at the Municipal Museum in Dresden. In 1944 his studio in Berlin was bombed by the Allies. After the Second World War, Felixmüller resumed teaching in Germany.

François Flameng (1856–1923) was a very successful French painter. The son of a celebrated engraver, he received a first-rate education in his craft. Flameng gained his reputation for his history painting and portraiture, and became a professor at the Academy of Fine Arts. He decorated important civic buildings including the Sorbonne and the Opera Comique, and designed France's first banknotes. In 1914 he was commissioned by the War Ministry and the magazine *l'Illustration* to produce an important series of war paintings, travelling regularly to the front. He was also made honorary president of the Society of Military Painters. For his services to art Flameng was granted France's highest civilian honour, the Legion d'Honneur.

Fritz Fuhrken (1894–1943), German expressionist painter and graphic artist, started his artistic career painting nature scenes. At the outbreak of war in 1914 he registered as a cadet, and by December 1917 was in the infantry on the Russian front in Galicia and Volhynia, where he continued to draw and paint. In August 1918, on the Somme front near Amiens, he was captured by the British and sent to an officers' prisoner-of-war camp in Yorkshire, where with several other artists he continued to explore a shared interest in expressionism.

Albert Henry Fullwood (1863–1930) grew up and studied in Birmingham, England, before emigrating to Sydney, Australia, in 1881. Soon after the First World War started, he joined the Allied Art Corps and became an Australian official war artist. He returned to Sydney in 1920 and worked chiefly in watercolour and etching.

Victor-Gabriel Gilbert (1847–1933), French painter of genre scenes, had his debut at the Paris Salon in 1873. He was highly respected for his fine detailed work, and his views of the colourful Parisian life, the boulevards, cafés and flower stalls became well known.

Colin Unwin Gill (1892–1940) was born at Bexley Heath in Kent and studied at the Slade School, where he won a Rome Scholarship in Decorative Painting in 1913, specialising in historical paintings. He served in France from 1915 to 1918, becoming an official war artist for the last year of the war. He became a member of the New English Art Club in 1926, after exhibiting with them for some years. In 1939 he moved to South Africa to paint a mural commission, but died before the work was completed.

Mary Riter Hamilton (1873–1954), Canadian painter, went to Paris in 1901 to study art, returning to Winnipeg in 1911 to mount a major exhibition of her work. After the First World War she obtained a publisher's commission to 'reproduce the battlefields in paint', and remained in Europe until 1922, producing over three hundred paintings, exhibited in Paris in 1922 and London in 1923. She subsequently donated most of her war paintings to the Public Archives of Canada.

Edward Harry Handley-Read (1870–1935), a popular magazine illustrator and military artist, was based in London. As well as military scenes, he painted extensively in Holland and in Venice.

John Hassall (1868–1948), English illustrator, was born in Kent and studied art at Newton Abbot College and in Heidelberg. After twice failing entry to The Royal Military Academy at Sandhurst, he emigrated to Manitoba in Canada in 1888, but returned to London two years later and continued his art studies in Antwerp and Paris, being much influenced by the work of Alphonse Mucha. In 1900 he opened the New Art School and School of Poster Design in Kensington.

William Hatherell (1855–1928), English painter and illustrator, grew up in London and studied art at the Royal Academy, where he exhibited from 1879, showing portraits, genre and illustrations. He worked for several British, Australian and American magazines as an illustrator.

Alfred Robert Hayward (1875–1971) was strongly influenced by the impressionists. Born in London, he studied art at the Royal College of Art and at the Slade School. During the period before 1914 Hayward travelled to West Indies, Central America and Italy, which he always loved. After serving in Artists' Rifles, Hayward was appointed an official war artist in 1918. By the end of the 1920s he was faring well as a painter, but his popularity dipped sharply in the 1930s.

Albert Heim (1849–1937), Swiss geologist and illustrator, was noted for his three-volume *Geologie der Schweiz*. Very early in life he became interested in the physical features of the Alps. In 1904 he was awarded the Wollaston medal by the Geological Society of London, and in 1905 he was made a member of the Royal Swedish Academy of Sciences.

Charles Gilbert Holiday (1879–1937), English illustrator, is best known for his studies of horses and horsemen. When war was declared in 1914 he worked as a war artist for *The Graphic*, and although too old to officially join up, in 1915 he obtained a commission into The Royal Field Artillery as an observation officer. He prepared a great many artillery panoramas, purchased by the Imperial War Museum as of 'considerable importance'. Holiday played an active part in drawing up plans of enemy positions, often venturing into no-man's land with his sketchbook. Some of his most haunting work resulted from his experiences at the Third Battle of Ypres.

Herbert Hughes-Stanton (1843–1914), English landscape painter, was born in London, the son of William Hughes, a still-life painter under whom he studied. He visited France regularly from 1906 to 1914, and served there as an official war artist, exhibiting work from this period at the Fine Art Society in 1919. He was knighted in 1923.

Richard Jack (1866–1952) was born in Sunderland in the north-east of England, and studied at the York School of Art before winning a scholarship to the Royal College of Art in 1866. In 1916 he accepted a commission in the Canadian Army to paint for the Canadian War Records Office, becoming Canada's first official war artist. A commissioned portrait of King George V was bought by the monarch himself, and he subsequently painted portraits of Queen Mary, King Alphonso of Spain, and various interiors at Buckingham Palace. Jack emigrated to Canada in 1938, where he painted landscapes as well as portraits.

Darsie Napier Japp (1883–1973) was born in Liverpool and took evening classes at the Lambeth School of Art under Philip Connard before studying at the Slade School from 1908 to 1909. He exhibited with the New English Art Club, becoming a member in 1919. After 1926 he spent most of his life abroad, in France, Spain and Portugal, where he died at Caixas.

George Kenner (1888–1971), born Georg Kennerknecht in Bavaria, studied in Germany and moved to London in 1910, where he worked as a process artist. He was registered as an alien enemy in August 1914, then abruptly interned five days after the RMS *Lusitania* was sunk by a German U-boat. He spent the war in internment camps in Surrey, London and the Isle of Man; in each, being a trained commercial artist and wanting to stay in practice with his work, he negotiated with the prisoner-of-war camp authorities to be allowed to create an extensive and important collection of internment scenes. Kenner was finally sent back to Germany in a prisoner exchange in March 1919, four months after the Armistice.

Eric Henry Kennington (1888–1960), English sculptor, artist and illustrator, was an official war artist in both world wars. He was born in London, the son of the well-known genre and portrait painter Thomas Benjamin Kennington, and was educated at St Paul's School and the Lambeth School of Art. In 1918 Kennington enlisted with the 13th (Kensington) Battalion London Regiment, and fought on the Western Front, but was wounded and discharged as unfit in June 1915. During his convalescence, he produced 'The Kensingtons at Laventie, Winter 1914', a portrait of a group of exhausted infantrymen, which caused a sensation. His work as a sculptor includes the memorial to the 24th Division in Battersea Park, and allegorical reliefs on the Shakespeare Memorial Theatre, Stratford upon Avon. Kennington again became an official war artist during the Second World War, commissioned to work for the Ministry of Information.

Ernst Ludwig Kirchner (1880–1938) was a German expressionist painter and printmaker and one of the founders of the artists' group Die Brücke (The Bridge), a key group leading to the foundation of expressionism. He volunteered for army service in 1918, but soon suffered a breakdown and was discharged. In 1933 his work was branded by the Nazis as degenerate, and in 1937 over six hundred of his works were sold or destroyed. In 1938 he committed suicide.

George Washington Thomas Lambert (1873–1930), Australian painter, was born in Russia where his English father was a working as a railway engineer; the family emigrated to Australia in 1887. Lambert attended art school in Sydney, and by 1914 was coming into prominence as a portrait painter and muralist In December 1917 he was appointed an official war artist with the honorary rank of lieutenant. He arrived at Alexandria, Egypt, in January 1918, and in January 1919 visited Gallipoli. His many meticulous and spirited sketches served as the foundation for four large battle-pictures now in the Australian War Memorial.

John Lavery (1856–1941) was born in Belfast, attended the Haldane Academy in Glasgow and the Académie Julian in Paris. In 1888 he was commissioned to paint the state visit of Queen Victoria to the Glasgow International Exhibition, which launched his career as a society painter. In 1909 Lavery married Hazel Martyn, an Irish-American known for her beauty and poise, who figures in more than four hundred of her husband's paintings. Lavery was appointed an official war artist in 1914, but ill health prevented him from travelling to France; he remained in Britain and painted the war effort on the home front.

Frederick William Leist (1878–1945) was an Australian artist who studied at the Sydney Art School under Julian Ashton, from whom he learned *plein air* techniques. During the First World War he was an official war artist with the Australian forces in Europe. After his war service he contributed two large murals for the Australian Exhibition at the British Empire Exhibition held at Wembley in 1924. As a result of these works Leist's popularity grew, and he gained several commissions from the United States.

Georges Paul Leroux (1877–1957), French landscape painter and illustrator, grew up and studied in Paris, and his early works featured the street life of that city. He later spent much time in Italy, winning the Grand Prix de Rome in 1904 and 1906. His patriotic paintings, particularly a large painting honouring the war dead of the city of Trelly, dominated his work between 1914 and 1919.

Arthur Lismer (1885–1969), English-born Canadian painter and a member of the Group of Seven, studied at the Academie Royale in Antwerp, where the Barbizon and post-impressionist movements were a key inspiration. In 1915 Lismer was commissioned as an official war artist. His best known work from the war years depicted what he observed and learned about in Halifax, Nova Scotia – minesweeping, convoying, patrolling and harbour defence.

Beatrice Ethel Lithiby (1889–1966), English artist and muralist, served in the Queen Mary's Army Auxiliary Corps, and was commissioned by the War Office to make drawings of the activities of the service.

John Hodgson Lobley (1878–1954), English artist, is best known for his work as an official war artist for the Royal Army Medical Corps during World War I. In addition to his wartime work, Lobley painted figures, portraits and landscapes.

William Frederick (Will) Longstaff (1879–1953) was an Australian painter and war artist best known for his works commemorating those who died in World War I. Born in Ballarat, Victoria, Longstaff studied art privately before joining the military and serving in the Boer War as a member of the South African Light Horse. At the outbreak of war in 1914 he enlisted in the Australian Imperial Force and was injured in the Gallipoli campaign. In October 1915 he joined a remount unit and served in France and Egypt before being evacuated to England in 1917. During his time in Egypt, Longstaff had made images of the Anzac Mounted Division and the other units. Upon his appointment as an official war artist in 1918 he produced numerous works during the final campaigns of the Western Front. After the war, Longstaff continued his art, turning many of his sketches into paintings.

Ambrose McEvoy (1878–1927)'s early works are landscapes and interiors with figures, in a style influenced by James McNeill Whistler, who spotted his talent early on. McEvoy enrolled at the Slade School when he was fifteen, where he was part of the group around Augustus John and William Orpen. During the First World War he was attached to the Royal Naval Division from 1916 to 1918, and painted a number of distinguished sailors and soldiers. In 1924 he was made an Associate of the Royal Academy and of the Royal Society of Portrait Painters, and of the Royal Watercolour Society in 1926.

Ludwig Meidner (1884–1966), studied at the Breslau Academy for Fine Art and the Applied arts before moving to Berlin. The instruction he took in etching from the artist Hermann Struck was important for his later career. In 1912 he started painting a series of 'apocalyptic landscapes', portraying the terror of the modern city in catastrophic settings. Conscripted into the military in 1916, Meidner served as an interpreter and censor at an internment camp for prisoners of war, continuing to produce portraits and scenes of camp life. Denounced as 'degenerate' in 1933 and persecuted because he was a Jew, in 1939 he fled with his family to England (his wife Else Meidner was also an artist), where he was interned as an enemy alien on the Isle of Man.

James Wilson Morrice (1865–1924) was a significant Canadian landscape painter. He studied at the Académie Julian in Paris, France, where he lived for most of his career, spending his winters in Canada painting snowy scenes. Shortly after the outbreak of war he left Paris for Canada, then with his health deteriorating he spent most of his time in Cuba and in Tangiers, where he died.

Olive Mudie-Cooke (1890–1953), English landscape and portrait artist, was deployed to France in 1916 with the First Aid Nursing Yeomanry, and in 1919 she was commissioned to produce a body of work by the Imperial War Museum's Women's Work Sub-Committee, set up to produce a record of the important war work done by women. Her stark and apocalyptic works featuring hospital and auxiliary staff depart from the 'official' fare of much commissioned work of the time.

John Northcote Nash (1893–1977) was a British painter of landscape and still life, wood-engraver and illustrator, and the younger brother of the artist Paul Nash. He grew up in London, and began painting in 1914. From November 1916 to January 1918 he served with the Artists' Rifles, and on the recommendation of his brother worked as an official war artist from 1918. His most famous painting is 'Over the Top', an image of the attack during which the 1st Battalion Artists' Rifles left their trenches and pushed towards Marcoing near Cambrai. Of the eighty men, sixty-eight were killed or wounded during the first few minutes. Nash was one of the twelve to be spared.

Paul Nash (1889–1946), British painter, surrealist, book illustrator and writer, was the older brother of the artist John Nash. At the outbreak of World War I, he reluctantly enlisted in the Artists' Rifles and was sent to the Western Front in February 1917 as a second lieutenant in the Hampshire Regiment. A few days before the Ypres offensive he fell into a trench, broke a rib and was invalided home. While recuperating, Nash worked from his front-line sketches to produce a series of drawings of the war, exhibited at the Goupil Gallery. As a result of this exhibition, Nash was recruited as an official war artist, and in November 1917 he returned to the Western Front where his drawings resulted in his first oil paintings.

Nash's paintings from this period are some of the most powerful and enduring images of the Great War painted by an English artist.

Christopher Richard Wynne (C.R.W.) Nevinson (1889–1946), one of the most famous war artists, was the son of the war correspondent and journalist Henry Nevinson and the suffrage campaigner and writer Margaret Nevinson. He studied at the St John's Wood School of Art and the Slade School. At the outbreak of war in 1914 Nevinson joined the Friends' Ambulance Unit with his father, and was deeply disturbed by his work tending wounded French soldiers. For a brief period he served as a volunteer ambulance driver before ill health soon forced his return to Britain. He used these experiences as the subject matter for a series of powerful paintings, on the basis of which he was eventually appointed as an official war artist, though his later paintings lacked the power of the earlier works. After the war Nevinson travelled to the USA, where he painted a number of powerful images of New York.

Emily Hilda (Rix) Nicholas (1884–1961), Australian artist, was born at Ballarat, Victoria, and educated at Merton Hall, Melbourne, and the National Gallery Schools' drawing class under Frederick McCubbin. From 1911 she had a studio in Paris, but she moved to England after the declaration of war. In October 1916 her new husband, George Nicholas, was killed in action at Flers, and in her grief she painted morbid images, symbolic of death and

sacrifice in war. Returning to Australia in 1918, Emily Nicholas painted heroic soldier images emphasising the spiritual aspects of war, which chimed with an emerging Anzac mythology and the identification of manhood with Australian nationhood.

William Newenham Montague Orpen (1878–1931), Irish painter and portraitist, was an official war artist during World War I. In 1917 he travelled to the Western Front and produced drawings and paintings of dead soldiers and German prisoners of war along with official portraits of generals and politicians. His large paintings of the Versailles Peace Conference captured the political wranglings of the gathered politicians and statesmen, whom Orpen came to loathe but relied upon for post-war commissions. He was deeply affected by the suffering he witnessed in the war; his 'To the Unknown British Soldier Killed in France', first exhibited in 1923, shows a flag-draped coffin flanked by a pair of ghostly and wretched soldiers clothed only in tattered blankets. Although widely admired by the public, this picture was attacked by the press, and Orpen painted out the soldiers before the painting was accepted by the Imperial War Museum.

Walter Stanley Paget (1863–1935), London-based English illustrator and brother of the more famous brothers Henry and Sidney, is best known for his illustrations of Thomas Hardy's novels and the Sherlock Holmes stories; he also produced a handful of paintings.

Harold Septimus Power (1877–1951) was a New-Zealand born Australian artist, and an official war artist for Australia in World War I. In 1899 he exhibited with the Melbourne Art Club, and soon after moved to Adelaide where he worked as an illustrator and political cartoonist. Between 1905 and 1907 Power studied at the Académie Julian in Paris, later settling in London. After war broke out in the summer of 1914, the Australian government appointed official war artists to depict the activities of the Australian Imperial Force in the European theatre of war – Power was appointed in 1917 and was attached to the 1st Division from September to December of that year and then again in August the following year. After the war Power was contracted by the Australian War Records Section for the next two decades.

Gilbert Rogers (c.1885–1940), a realist English painter, grew up in Liverpool. At the end of hostilities in 1918 he was put in charge of a team of thirteen artists set to work in a London studio by Lt. Col. F.S. Brereton, as chairman of a Committee for the Medical History of the War, to record the work of medical staff on the front line. Rogers' detailed canvasses are notable for their power and honesty.

William Rothenstein (1872–1945), English society painter, draughtsman and writer on art, was born into a German-Jewish family in Bradford, West Yorkshire. He is best known for his portrait drawings of famous people; he was an official war artist in both the First and Second World Wars.

George 'AE' Russell (1867–1935) *see* page 206.

Frank Earle Schoonover (1877–1972) was a prolific and accomplished American illustrator who studied under Howard Pyle at the Drexel Institute in Philadelphia, and became part of the Brandywine School. A regular contributor to books and magazines during the early twentieth century, in 1918 and 1919 he produced a series of paintings featuring American soldiers for souvenir prints published in the *Ladies' Home Journal*. He died at 94, leaving behind more than two thousand illustrations.

Felix Schwormstädt (1870–1938), German painter, draftsman, and illustrator, made his name as a marine artist. He became one of the star illustrators of the popular illustrated magazine *Illustrirte Zeitung*, where his strikingly realistic illustrations were published in almost every issue.

George Bertin Scott (1873–1943) was a French war correspondent and illustrator for the French magazine *l'Illustration*. He is noted for his paintings of the Balkan Wars and the First World War, also covering the Spanish Civil War and the early years of the Second World War. One of his major works, an oil painting of his depicting King Constantine I of Greece during the Balkan Wars, hangs in the Presidential Palace in Athens.

Charles Sims (1873–1928) received his art education in London in the South Kensington and Royal Academy Schools, and in Paris in the ateliers of Julian and Baschet. He was elected Associate of the Royal Academy in 1908, Associate of the Royal Watercolour Society in 1911, Member of the Royal Watercolour Society in 1914 and Royal Academician in 1915. The First World War proved to be a traumatic experience for Sims, from which he never recovered. His eldest son was killed, and he was deeply disturbed by what he witnessed in France where he was sent as a war artist in 1918. He committed suicide in 1928.

John Singer Sargent (1856–1925), the leading American artist of his day, is best known for his evocations of Edwardian luxury. By the outbreak of war in 1914 he had almost stopped painting, having officially closed his studio in 1907, but he did agree to serve briefly as an official war artist in 1918, producing several powerful canvasses.

Austin Osman Spare (1886–1956) was an English artist and occultist. His art is known for its clear use of line and its depictions of monstrous imagery. He studied at the Royal College of Art in South Kensington and trained as a draughtsman, while also taking a personal interest in Theosophy and the western esoteric tradition, becoming briefly involved with Aleister Crowley. After publishing a briefly-lived art magazine, Form, he was conscripted in 1914 and worked as an official war artist.

Inglis Sheldon-Williams (1870–1940) was born in Hampshire, the son of a landscape painter. He moved to Canada in 1887, returning to England in 1891 to study art. He travelled extensively in South Africa, India and Europe before returning to Canada in 1913 as a mature artist. In October 1918, he went to the front in Europe as an official Canadian war artist.

John William Thomason, Jr (1893–1944) was a Lieutenant Colonel in the United States Marine Corps, as well as an author and illustrator of several books and magazine stories. During the First World War he served as the executive officer of the 49th Company, 1st Battalion, 5th Marine Regiment, and was awarded the Navy Cross.

Henry Tonks (1862–1937), born in Birmingham, England, was a draughtsman, illustrator and surgeon, studying first medicine and later art. From 1892 he taught at the Slade School of Fine Art, where his pupils included Augustus John, Stanley Spencer and Rex Whistler. Tonks was an official war artist towards the end of World War I, and accompanied John Singer Sargent on tours of the Western Front. In August 1918 they witnessed a field of wounded men near Le Bac du Sud, Doullens, which became the basis for Sargent's vast canvas 'Gassed'.

William Thurston Topham (1888–1966), artist and architect, was born in England and started painting when he moved to Montreal in Canada in 1910. He was a war artist in both world wars, in the second working with the 1st Canadian Siege Battery.

Harry Everett Townsend (1879–1941), American artist and illustrator, was a war artist for the United States Army during World War I. In 1912 he established a studio in northern France so that he could be close to both Paris and London. The onset of war forced Townsend to return to the United States, where he resumed his work as an illustrator. He began his war service drawing posters before receiving his captain's commission in 1918. As a war artist he produced powerful images showing how the rigours of combat leave little to distinguish between winners and losers.

Félix Edouard Vallotton (1865–1925) was a Swiss painter and printmaker associated with the development of the modern woodcut. In 1914 he responded to the war by volunteering for the French army, but he was rejected because of his age, and instead expressed his feelings for his adopted country in the woodcut series *This is War*. He subsequently spent three weeks on a tour of the Champagne front in 1917, on a commission from the Ministry of Fine Arts.

Frederick Horsman Varley (1881–1969), a member of the Canadian Group of Seven artists, was born in Sheffield, England, and studied art in Sheffield and in Belgium. He moved to Canada in 1912 on the advice of another Sheffield artist, Arthur Lismer. His work came to the attention of Lord Beaverbrook, who arranged for him to be commissioned as an official war artist, and he accompanied Canadian troops in the Hundred Days offensive from Amiens to Mons. Although he had been enthusiastic to travel to France as a war artist, he was deeply disturbed by what he saw, and his contribution in the war influenced the work of the Group of Seven, who often chose to paint Canadian wilderness that had been damaged by fire or harsh climates.

Louis Weirter (Whirter) (1873–1932) was born in Edinburgh and studied at the Royal Scottish Academy Schools and in Paris. He is best known for his pictures of World War I, but he also produced many of architectural paintings and etchings, as well as illustrating a number of travel books.

Norman Wilkinson (1878–1971) was born in Cambridge, England, and his initial training was musical. He was a chorister at St Paul's Cathedral Choir School from the age of 8 to 14 but he switched to Portsmouth Art School. He started work as an illustrator and poster artist, his work appearing in *The Illustrated London News* from 1898 to 1915. In the First World War he served in The Royal Naval Volunteer Regiment as a lieutenant. He painted in both oils and watercolours, concentrating mainly on marine subjects and landscapes. His work was exhibited at the Royal Academy and commercially at The Fine Art Society in London.

Harold Sandys Williamson (1892–1978) was born in Yorkshire and studied at the Leeds School of Art. At the outbreak of war in 1914 he attempted to enlist in the army, but was turned down on health grounds. In 1916 he was accepted as a rifleman and was injured at the Battle of Delville Wood. Whilst recuperating he was recruited to the War Artists Scheme for the Ministry of Information, but the Armistice meant that the contract was not taken up. After the war he designed posters for several commercial organisations including London Transport.

Gert H. Wollheim (1894–1974), German expressionist painter, was born in Dresden and studied in Weimar. During the First World War he fought on the Eastern and Western Fronts and was wounded in the stomach, an experience which became crucial for his later artwork. His work is violent and contorted, and stresses the element of the grotesque. In 1919 he left Berlin for Düsseldorf, where he created a large number of woodcuts, etchings, and paintings to express his terrible experiences of war. The monumental triptych 'The Wounded' has the figure of a soldier in the position of the crucified Jesus, with a lacerated belly, as its centrepiece.

Stanley Llewelyn Wood (1867–1928), a British-born illustrator who emigrated to Kansas in 1879, was a prolific contributor to news and boys' magazines and illustrated novels.

INDEX OF FIRST LINES

ACKNOWLEDGEMENTS

EDITOR'S ACKNOWLEDGEMENTS

The credit for the brilliant idea of producing a volume of poetry of the Great War, drawing on the writers of six nations, and illustrating it with paintings by the artists of these nations, goes to John Button of Bookcraft. John also compiled the artists' biographies.

When the project was suggested to me it was immediately appealing. However, the limitations of my own knowledge and abilities in relation to the vast task before me soon became apparent. I had not realised the extent to which this book would be breaking new ground. It seems that outside of Britain the poetry of the Great War is of small concern, and little is read or published. Poets of great merit are, for the most part, unknown. Within Britain, published war poetry from other nations is sparse and, in the case of German and French poetry translated into English, there is almost nothing at all. I, and the readers of this book, are therefore greatly indebted to the translators of the French and German poetry, especially to Ian Higgins and Patrick Bridgwater, without whose groundbreaking research and scholarship this volume would not have been possible.

I am also greatly indebted to Julie Laws of Bookcraft for her considerable work as picture researcher for this book, and to Duncan Rogers for his expert, critical and insightful reading of my introduction.

POETRY ACKNOWLEDGEMENTS

Laurence Binyon, 'For the Fallen' (by permission of The Society of Authors, literary representatives of the Estate of Laurence Binyon).

Siegfried Sassoon, 'Does it Matter?', 'The General', 'Great Men', 'Memorial Tablet', 'Everyone Sang' (© Siegfried Sassoon by permission of the Estate of George Sassoon).

Edmund Blunden, 'Report on Experience' (from *Selected Poems*, by permission of Carcanet Press).

Robert Nichols, 'Noon', 'Eve of Assault: Infantry Going Down to Trenches', 'The Day's March', 'Dawn on the Somme' (by permission of Mrs Anne Charlton).

Alfred Noyes, 'The Victory Ball' (by permission of The Society of Authors, literary representatives of the estate of Alfred Noyes).

Robert Graves, 'Armistice Day, 1918' *(from Complete Poems in One Volume*, by permission of Carcanet Press)

Vera Brittain, 'Perhaps' (by permission of Mark Bostridge and T.J. Brittain-Catlin, literary executors for the Estate of Vera Brittain).

Herbert Asquith, 'Fallen Subaltern', 'Nightfall' (by permission of Roland Asquith).

John Hewitt, 'Nineteen Sixteen, or the Terrible Beauty' (by permission of Dr J.K. Millar).

Lord Dunsany, 'To the Fallen Irish Soldiers' (by permission of Curtis Brown Group Ltd, London on behalf of The Dunsany Literary Trust, © Lord Dunsany, 1929).

Vance Palmer, 'Who Being Dead …', 'Romance', 'The Farmer Remembers the Somme', 'The Harvest' (by permission of the Estate of Edward Vance Palmer).

Elspeth Honeyman, 'Canada's Answer' (by permission of Elspeth Probyn and Jane Probyn).

Robert Service, 'The Stretcher-Bearer', 'Faith', 'The Lark', 'The Mourners', 'Pilgrims' (by permission of Anne Longepe).

Frank Prewett, 'The Soldier', 'The Survivor' (by permission of W.G. Prewett).

Anton Schnack, 'The Dead Soldier', 'In the Trenches', 'Standing To' (© Elfenbein Verlag, Berlin. Translations from Anton Schnack: *Werke in zwei Bänden*, edited by Hartmut Vollmer, 2003).

Translation of 'Journey by Night' (by permission of Francis Clark-Lowes and Mike Sharon).

Translations of 'Hymn One, from Five Hymns, August 1914', 'Suppose War is Coming', 'Leaving for the Front', 'Prayer Before Battle', 'The Battle of Saarburg', 'At the Beginning of the War', 'Flares Climb High', 'War', 'Baptism of Fire', 'I Did Not Like', 'Dance of Death, 1916', 'Dying', 'A Field Hospital', 'Deserted House', 'Evening at the Front', 'At the Front', 'The Dead Soldier', 'In the Trenches', 'Standing To' (by permission of Patrick Bridgwater).

Translations of 'Offering', 'Veni, Sancte Spiritus!', 'To Norman Lads', 'Gamecocks', 'Mobilisation', 'I Always Thought …', 'The North Wind …', 'Nocturne', 'Market', 'Young Shades', 'To Cam', 'Undermanned', 'All Souls' Day' (by permission of Ian Higgins).

Translation of 'De Profundis' (by permission of Graham Dunstan Martin).

Translation of 'Grodek' (by permission of Richard Hamburger on behalf of the Michael Hamburger Trust).

Translations of 'The Soldier's Soliloquies' and 'By Evening's Blue-Grey Threshold … ' (by permission of Berit Owen).

Painting Acknowledgements

Unless otherwise credited, the original paintings in this volume can be found in the national public archives listed below. Very many of the paintings were commissioned by national government agencies from artists in the capacity of 'official war artists', this status varying from government to government and over time. Few of the paintings are on open public display, though the museums in question regularly organise themed exhibitions.

Australian War Memorial, Canberra   www.awm.gov.au

Page 99, Frank Crozier, 'On the Way', AWM 2159; page 108, Fred Leist, 'Australian Infantry Attack in Polygon Wood', AWM 02927; page 111, H. Septimus Power, 'Third Ypres, July 31st, 1917; Taking the Guns Through', AWM 3330; page 119, Will Longstaff, 'Menin Gate at Midnight (The Ghosts of Menin Gate)', AWM 9807; page 120, Hilda Rix Nicholas, 'A Mother of France', AWM 3281; page 122, Will Longstaff, '8th August, 1918', AWM 03022.

Canadian War Museum, Ottawa   www.warmuseum.ca

Page 16, William Thurston Topham, 'Moonrise Over Mametz Wood', CWM 19710261-0752; page 35, James Morrice, 'Canadians in the Snow', CWM 8949; page 37, Alfred Bastien, 'Over the Top, Neuville-Vitasse', CWM 8058; page 47, Alfred Bastien, 'Canadian Gunners in the Mud, Passchendaele', CWM 8095; page 62, Frederick H. Varley, 'German Prisoners', CWM 8961; page 76, Richard Jack, 'The Second Battle of Ypres, April 22nd–May 25th, 1915', CWM 8179; page 85, Maurice Cullen, 'The Cambrai Road'; page 89, William Thurston Topham, 'The Artist's Own Dug-out on the Albert-Braye Roadside', CWM 19710261-0755; page 91, Arthur Lismer, 'Sketch for "Minesweepers and Seaplanes"', CWM 19710261-6421; page 123, Norman Wilkinson, 'Canada's Answer', CWM 8934; page 124, C.R.W. Nevinson, 'War in the Air', CWM 8651; page 125, Edgar Bundy, 'Landing of the First Canadian Division at Saint-Nazaire', CWM 8121; page 128, Colin Unwin Gill, 'Canadian Observation Post'; page 129, Frederick H. Varley, 'For What?', CWM 8911; page 130, Alfred Bastien, 'Canadian Sentry, Moonlight, Neuville-Vitesse'; page 131, Maurice Cullen, 'No Man's Land', CWM 19710261-0134; page 135, Eric Henry Kennington, 'The Conquerors', CWM 8968; page 139, Cyril Barraud, 'The Stretcher-Bearer Party', CWM 8021; page 143, Charles Sims, 'Sacrifice', CWM 8802; page 144, Frederick H. Varley, 'Some Day the People Will Return', CWM 8910; page 145, Inglis Sheldon-Williams, 'The Return to Mons', CWM 8969; page 181, Douglas W. Culham, 'Mud Road to Passchendaele'.

Imperial War Museum, London   www.iwm.org.uk

Page 2, Paul Nash, 'Ruined Country: Old Battlefield, Vimy, near La Folie Wood', IWM ART 721; page 18, Darsie Japp, 'Regimental Band', IWM ART 4031; page 19, Colin Unwin Gill, 'A Gunner', IWM ART 2281; page 25, Eric Henry Kennington, 'Gassed and Wounded', IWM ART 4744; page 26, Paul Nash, 'The Ypres Salient at Night', IWM ART 1145; page 31, John Nash, 'Over the Top', IWM 1656; page 33, Cecil Aldin, 'A Land Girl Ploughing', IWM ART 2618; page 43, Beatrice Lithiby, 'YWCA Hut for the Queen Mary's Army Auxiliary Corps, Le Havre', IWM ART 2907; page 45, Charles Sims, 'The Old German Front Line, Arras', IWM ART 2282; page 52, Gilbert Rogers, 'Gassed, "In Arduis Fidelis"', IWM 3819; page 53, John Singer Sargent, 'Gassed', IWM ART 1460; page 59, C.R.W. Nevinson, 'Paths of Glory', IWM ART 518; page 61, John Hodgson Lobley, 'Loading Wounded at Boulogne', IWM 2760; page 65, Paul Nash, 'The Mule Track', IWM 1153; page 74, John Lavery, 'The Fore-Cabin of HMS *Queen Elizabeth*', IWM ART 4219; page 78, Ambrose McEvoy, 'One of the Nelsons', IWM ART 1328; page 80, Ambrose McEvoy, 'Bourlon Wood, Somme', IWM ART 1338; page 83, John Hassall, 'The Vision of St George over the Battlefield', IWM ART 15600; page 87, Alfred Hayward, 'The Soldiers' Buffet, Charing Cross Station', IWM ART 1882; page 96, William Hatherell, 'Nurse, Wounded Soldier and Child', IWM ART 5194; page 97, Olive Mudie-Cooke, 'Etaples: British Military Cemetery', IWM ART 5404; page 104, Henry Tonks, 'An Advanced Dressing Station in France', IWM 1922; page 115, Charles Ernest Butler, 'Blood and Iron', IWM ART 6492; page 133, Gilbert Rogers, 'Mud', IWM ART 3734; page 138, Gilbert Rogers, 'An RAMC Stretcher-Bearer', IWM ART 3775; page 147, C.R.W. Nevinson, 'The Road from Arras to Bapaume', IWM ART 516; page 165, Colin Unwin Gill, 'Heavy Artillery', IWM ART 2274; page 180, E. Handley-Read, 'An Observer', IWM ART 178; page 198, George Kenner, 'Storm and Rainbow, Symbol for Near End of War 1918', IWM ART 17055; page 197, Colin Unwin Gill, 'Evening, After a Push', IWM ART 1210; page 203, Harold Sandys Williamson, 'A German Attack on a Wet Morning, April 1918', IWM ART 1986; front cover, John Lavery, 'The Cemetery, Etaples, 1919', IWM 2884.

Archives New Zealand   archives.govt.nz

Page 101, George Edmund Butler, 'At the Alert, Gas Zone', AAAC 898 NCWA Q458; page 103, Charles Dixon, 'The Landing at Anzac', AAAC 898 NCWA Q388; page 106, Walter Armiger Bowring, 'The Homecoming from Gallipoli', AAAC 898 NCWA 532; page 117, George Edmund Butler, 'A Roadside Cemetery near Neuve Eglise', AAAC 898 NCWA 471; page 121, George Edmund Butler, 'Butte de Polygon', AAAC 898 NCWA 456; page 156, George Edmund Butler, 'Burial Party at Bellevue near Solesnes', AAAC 898 NCWA 477.

The publishers are grateful to the following artists or their estates for their assistance and permission to use their work:
Paul Williamson for Harold Sandys Williamson, 'A German Attack on a Wet Morning, April 1918' (page 203).
Christa Kenner Bedford for George Kenner, 'Storm and Rainbow, Symbol for Near End of War 1918' (page 198).
DACS for paintings by Otto Dix (© DACS 2012).